The Faces of
Contemporary
Cities

The Faces of Contemporary Cities

Edited by
Davide Ponzini

New York · Paris · London · Milan

Table of Contents

P. 6   PREFACE
Liam Cummins interviewed by Davide Ponzini

P. 10   INTRODUCTION
The faces of contemporary cities and the transnational circulation of architectural technologies
Davide Ponzini

P. 24   New York

P. 36   CHAPTER 1
Contemporary architecture to the test of the history of constructors
Paolo Scrivano

P. 48   London

P. 60   CHAPTER 2
Digital mass-customization and the rise of the nonstandard architectural envelope
Mario Carpo

P. 72   Paris
P. 82   Frankfurt

P. 90   CHAPTER 3
The assemblage of city faces: Transnational networks, architectural projects, and urban effects
Davide Ponzini

P. 104   Hong Kong
P. 114   Shanghai

P. 124   CHAPTER 4

Networks of architectural production: Behind the façade of Hamburg's Elbphilharmonie
Johannes Dreher and Joachim Thiel

P. 136   Sydney

P. 144   CHAPTER 5

Transnational histories and geographies of the Permasteelisa Group, 1973–2022
Marco Antonio Minozzo Gabriel

P. 154   SELECTED PROJECTS

SAS Royal Hotel P. 156
Copenhagen, 1960

Sydney Opera House P. 160
Sydney, 1973

Lloyd's Building P. 164
London, 1986

Bank of China Tower P. 170
Hong Kong, 1990

Guggenheim Museum Bilbao P. 176
Bilbao, 1997

Glòries Tower P. 182
Barcelona, 2005

Hearst Tower P. 186
New York, 2006

HQ Building P. 190
Abu Dhabi, 2010

The Shard P. 194
London, 2012

UniCredit Tower P. 200
Milan, 2012

Elbphilharmonie P. 206
Hamburg, 2016

M+ P. 210
Hong Kong, 2021

P. 216   APPENDIX

About the authors P. 218

References P. 220

Photo credits P. 223

Liam Cummins
(CEO, Permasteelisa Group)
interviewed by the editor of the book,
Davide Ponzini

Davide Ponzini: *This book investigates the roles of design technology providers in transforming the face of contemporary cities. On the occasion of its fiftieth anniversary, I led a multidisciplinary group of scholars to explore the histories and geographies of the Permasteelisa Group—a multinational that has supported the design and construction of many iconic buildings and areas in dozens of cities around the world. Through the findings, maps, and photographs presented in this book, the reader can better understand and literally see the urban effects resulting from the availability and transfer of Permasteelisa-provided technologies and solutions over several decades and in multiple urban settings. How do you interpret the long-lasting relationship of the Permasteelisa Group's companies with cities around the world?*

Liam Cummins: The long-standing relationship between the Permasteelisa Group and cities worldwide can be interpreted as a testament to the Group's commitment to architectural excellence and urban development. Permasteelisa Group's extensive portfolio of iconic projects, ranging from skyscrapers to cultural landmarks, showcases our pivotal role in shaping the urban landscapes of many cities. Our close relationships with some of the world's greatest architects demonstrate our transnational team's ability to translate their visionary ideas into tangible, engineered solutions. This exemplifies Permasteelisa's dedication to enhancing the aesthetic and functional aspects of cities, ultimately contributing to the growth and identity of these urban centers on a global scale.

DP: *Do you see this role as part of the wider contributions that the Group's expertise can provide to contemporary architecture and today's cities? Do you think that this extends the Group's civic responsibility?*

LC: Yes, the Permasteelisa Group has a significant track record in successfully leveraging its expertise in complex architecture and urban development projects. Our ability to consistently deliver innovative and sustainable solutions in iconic projects contributes to the advancement of architectural standards and urban aesthetics.

This extends the Group's civic responsibility by demonstrating our commitment to enhancing the quality of life within cities and ensuring safe, livable, and sustainable urban environments. In doing so, the Permasteelisa Group plays a vital role in shaping the future of cities, not only as a leader in architectural solutions but also as a responsible entity committed to the betterment of urban spaces.

DP: *The book reports, from different angles, the history of the Group over the last fifty years, as in 2023 you celebrate the anniversary of the creation of its parent company ISA. It brings together the various histories of the companies, like Permasteel, Gartner, and Scheldebouw, that merged into the Group. This is a way to read the broader as well as the more articulated operations of this technology provider group over time. Looking back on these five decades, how do you frame the Group's heritage and how does it affect its organization and progress? How has this "company of companies" been evolving in recent years and how does the transnational soul of the Group affect its contributions in different cities?*

LC: Over the past five decades, the Permasteelisa Group has built on a rich heritage rooted in the merging, over time, of three unique companies: Permasteelisa, born from the acquisition of the Australian Permasteel by ISA, Gartner, and Scheldebouw. As a "company of companies," it has leveraged the unique nature, expertise, and brand of all three to create a culture of collaboration, diversity, and a commitment to technical excellence. This heritage provides the Group with cross-disciplinary expertise, adaptability, and a global perspective. Recent years have seen the Group evolve by embracing new technological and sustainability advancements, critical in contemporary architecture and city development. Moreover, Permasteelisa Group's global presence allows it to draw inspiration from diverse cultural influences and adapt solutions to local urban environments. This cultural sensitivity and transnational perspective enable the Group as a whole to create architectural solutions that resonate with the unique identities and needs of each city.

DP: *The book focuses on the transnational nature of Permasteelisa's trajectory and operations, expanding its scope from Northern Italy to Australia and Asia, to Europe, North America, and the Middle East. How do these cooperation links support the presence of the Group in specific places and improve its ability to have an impact?*

LC: Permasteelisa Group's global footprint and organizational structure increase its capacity to make a significant impact by enabling agile adaptation to diverse markets and geopolitical landscapes. This facilitates the transfer of our technologies across our branches, the exchange of global best practices, the utilization of local expertise, and the cultivation of strong relationships with local stakeholders. Consequently, the Group can tailor its architectural solutions to align with regional nuances, improve project quality through cross-border knowledge sharing, and navigate complex regulatory environments, ultimately enhancing its effectiveness and influence in various urban environments across the globe.

DP: *Given this historical evolution and geographical complexity, why engage with academic research that focuses on your own practice now? What do you see in this book, besides the outcome of our research?*

LC: This commitment to research—on the occasion of the Group's fiftieth anniversary—helps us raise awareness regarding our own operations from an architectural, urban, and transnational perspective.

In particular, we are interested in generating and portending a more systematic understanding of our contribution to city transformation. In other words, to expose our impact beyond the support of architectural design firms. Our long-term contribution in specific settings—like the seven cities analyzed in this book—shows the additional value we repeatedly brought to the design and development process and how this contribution composes at the urban scale over time. This critical understanding will nurture our corporate culture and attitude to evolve and constantly improve our bespoke solutions.

The Group decided to have independent experts analyze its work and its role in transforming cities as part of our corporate social responsibility strategy. More generally this is part of our vision for our Group's future and cultural mission as a leading design technology provider in the world.

By generating and sharing research-based knowledge and more advanced interpretations of urban transformation, we seek to improve not only our own business but also future changes in the built environment, urban places, and our society at large.

Of course, the book is intended to please the eye and engage with a non-academic audience that is interested in design, architecture, engineering, technology, and the future of our cities. This is a way to show the roles we play, reach out to different actors and groups, and expand our potential further.

DP: *As you mentioned, the Group counts on repeat cooperation with the world's most advanced engineering companies, as well as important architecture firms. Simi-*

larly, multinational developers and contractors have also collaborated with you repeatedly. What are the challenges—technological, architectural, urban, or otherwise—for the Permasteelisa Group to keep thriving in the future?

LC: I see the Permasteelisa Group facing three key challenges in the future: sustainability, technological innovation, and evolving urban landscapes. Firstly, sustainability considerations are paramount as the construction industry is at the forefront of the fight against climate change. The Group must prioritize eco-friendly practices, materials, and energy-efficient designs such as our Closed Cavity Façade (CCF) solutions. Permasteelisa Group's future success hinges on its ability to invest in sustainable architectural solutions and integrate sustainability at the core of every project.

Secondly, the Group must continually invest in cutting-edge technologies to remain at the forefront of the industry. This includes advancements in materials, automation, artificial intelligence, and digital design tools, all of which are integral to creating architecturally innovative and efficient solutions. Embracing digitalization will be vital for streamlining design and manufacturing processes.

Lastly, the evolving urban landscape poses challenges in the form of population growth, urban development, and climate change. To address these issues, our Group must design solutions that promote urban resilience, sustainable living, and community well-being. This requires the ability to adapt architectural designs to meet the unique challenges posed by different cities and regions.

Overall, navigating these technological, sustainable, and urban challenges will be essential for Permasteelisa Group's continued success and influence in the architectural and construction industries as well as for its contribution to changing the face of contemporary cities.

Davide Ponzini

The faces of contemporary cities and the transnational circulation of architectural technologies

Our way of observing and understanding the world often starts from its surface. We tend to first recognize the people around us by their appearance and facial features. Just as someone's face does not tell us the entire history or character of a person, neither can we expect this from a complex composition like a city. Even if we frequently recognize one city through key images—an iconic building, a square, or the skyline—we cannot necessarily claim to know its deeper characteristics or historic evolution. This book shows how the built environment and the creation of its material surfaces can help to better understand processes of urban transformation and architecture more generally. The research behind this book interprets the material dimension of buildings and the built environment as the product of multiple networks of skills and transnational sociopolitical relationships, revealing the connections among cities and their transforming agents to explore, in particular, the role of designers and design technology providers over time.

The faces of cities

The title of this book borrows the title of an essay by Ludovico Quaroni, "Il Volto della Città" ["The Face of the City"] (1954), and reinterprets it from a contemporary perspective. Quaroni gives the example of how the focus on monuments—by tourists as much as by some urban planners and scholars—only partially captures the sense of place and the city evolution. To understand the faces of a city, even those represented by the most distinctive and iconic monuments, it is necessary to understand both the monuments and the urban fabric they are part of. I personally see in Quaroni's writing an acute anticipation of what has been developing in more recent years as assemblage, which I will discuss further. For this reason, I have taken the license to use a variation on his title.

Obviously, there are past books that have documented the transformation of a city, using the same metaphor of the faces of the city; for example, the book *The Face of New York* (Feininger and Lyman, 1954) offers a historical analysis of important places, infrastructure, and ways of living in New York. The text and the iconographic analysis demonstrate an important effort, which however has a documentary and not an interpretative objective.

FACING THE CITY The faces of contemporary cities emerge from landmarks—like the One World Trade Center and Eight Spruce Street buildings in this picture of Manhattan—as well as city fabrics, urban life, and imaginaries. The images in this book document, analyze, and display some of these faces.

Even the analysis of cities such as London or Paris (Clunn, 1933a and 1933b) historically and visually documents the growth and transformation of a single city. Books of this kind continue today to tell the story of the evolution of cities. There is no shortage of research that analyzes the evolution of cities in light of major economic, social, and environmental trends. However, they rarely dwell on the forms and contextual processes that influence them (Ponzini, 2020). Mainstream architectural history has a limited spectrum. On the one hand, it tends to study notable buildings, often iconic or representative of a given style or era. On the other hand, the insights are important from a disciplinary point of view and generally refer to architects' "authorial" work. In this cultural context, contemporary media—both online and offline—continuously provide snapshots that circulate project images, often limited to glorifying the work of architects and, to a lesser extent, the other professions involved (engineers, developers, investors). Rarely do they critically explain how this work contributes, positively or negatively, to the long-term evolution of cities and local societies. Past authors and research groups have delved into the economic and sociopolitical context of architectural and urban planning to help better understand the work of architects in relation to the system of economic interests and agents. In this chapter, there is not enough room for a review of the literature and approaches in the field. It is sufficient to mention that scholars from various disciplines, such as Manfredo Tafuri (1973), Jane M. Jacobs (2003), and Leslie Sklair (2017), have investigated how certain urban forms have consolidated in the Western world and in other emerging countries due to the economic, financial, and cultural mechanisms that support them. These interpretative efforts have used the buildings to highlight networks of interests, to question dynamics of transformation of cities and society. Such investigations are hugely important, but they tend to formulate general theories ill-suited for understanding the contingent transformations in a specific city and place.

City faces as assemblage

While considering various cities and well-known projects, this book does not intend to document the evolution of cities or the work of one type of expert (architects or others) but rather to explore, for the first time, a specific proposition. The face of contemporary cities is an assemblage where buildings emphasize distinctive features of the city, and they would not have the same meaning and recognition if they were isolated from their physical and socioeconomic context. The connection with the local context and with other projects and places that are geographically distant makes the similarities and differences among the cities more evident. Within this framework, one can recognize the role and contribution not only of architects and urban planners but also of design technology providers in transforming the face of cities.

To explore this proposition, I have adopted an approach inspired by the theoretical work of Bruno Latour (2005). Interpreting architecture and cities as socio-material assemblages (Farias and Bender, 2010; Jacobs and Merriam, 2011; Lieto and Beauregard, 2015; Yaneva, 2017) allows us to delve into the materiality of the built environment and trace the connections between different networks of actors and places. Without going too far into the theory, I maintain that through this approach one can better observe the faces of cities and understand not only their physical and symbolic components but also how these depend on certain networks of actors as well as their historical and contingent evolution in given places of the world. The existence of iconic buildings and even their success depend on a much larger network of experts, policy makers, and users than the architecture firm alone (Alaily-Mattar et al. 2020). In this sense, the buildings themselves can be seen as contingent assemblages of expertise, ideas, projects, materials, and social uses that are meaningful and recognizable as part of a broader urban landscape. My colleague Harvey Molotch and I (Molotch and Ponzini, 2019 and 2022) coined the motto: "follow the building" and showed the transnational assemblages of iconic buildings and central places in various cities.

The representation of the faces of the cities inevitably requires simplification inherent to the tools with which we are most accustomed. As far as photography is concerned, the skyline provides a synthetic image of a group of buildings in which the urban fabric is not visible or relevant (Nastasi, 2016). Bird's-eye views typically emphasize the elevation of buildings and their vertical geometry while potentially providing a wealth of information and insight into the structure of the city and its functioning at the ground level. Street-level photography is ambivalent. On the one hand, it depicts the geometries of buildings or their technical and aesthetic features—in architecture media canonically devoid of any human presence. On the other hand, these images can be a formidable tool for analysis and interpretation of city life at the intersection and interaction between the human and the material.

Observing the contemporary result of the historical stratification of these interactions between social networks and the built environment suggests that it is a socio-material complex that generates the image and the urban experience, in other words, what I call the face of the city in this book. For this reason we included detailed maps and 3D representations of projects completed by the Permasteelisa Group within specific areas and neighborhoods (see page 16). This perspective shifts attention from individual iconic buildings to the complex urban systems they are part of. Furthermore, this perspective starts questioning the authorship of architects as the main agents of the transformation of an area. However, the information about the main design firm is reported for each building not only to help read-

Davide Ponzini

The faces of contemporary cities and the transnational circulation of architectural technologies

ers recognize the projects but also to show the recurrence of certain partnerships between leading international firms and Permasteelisa Group's companies in the same city over time and across cities. Obviously, this is just a first step to broaden the field of recognition and responsibility of those who design and construct buildings and cities beyond the architect and urban planner. The faces of contemporary cities derive from processes in which iconic buildings can be the most recognizable elements—the focal points of our gaze—that are nonetheless influenced by the surrounding urban fabric (not only buildings but also open spaces, infrastructure, etc.) as well as by the ways that local communities, city users, and global populations of tourists and workers use and perceive these places and their images. The multiscalar and multidimensional understanding of these city faces is useful to overcome a mere visual conception and to shift attention toward the composition of the identity of places and symbols that are increasingly losing their civic meaning (Nicolin, 2012). This approach also allows one to connect the images of these faces beyond the scale of a single city and compare them with other cities and deepen their interconnections over time.

Fifty years of the Permasteelisa Group

The occasion for these reflections derives from a request to deepen—thanks to the methods developed at the Politecnico di Milano TAU-Lab and to a selected group of researchers—the work of the Permasteelisa Group, which in 2023 celebrates the fiftieth anniversary of the parent company's foundation (ISA–Infissi Serramenti in Alluminio). The historic period is sufficiently long and particularly significant to deepen the transnational expertise network and connections among projects in various cities of the world. The 1973–2022 period saw an unprecedented process of globalization, from overcoming the 1970s oil crisis to the uncertainty caused by the Covid-19 pandemic and the geopolitical developments of the war in Ukraine. In this period, there has been an intensification of political, commercial, and cultural relations on a global scale and the composition of a market system that, for better or worse, has overcome national barriers and transformed contemporary societies and cities. This

BIRD'S-EYE VIEW OF THE CITY OF LONDON
The bird's-eye view shows the ensemble of buildings and places. Its perspective effect emphasizes vertical components in the built environment and this is why it has become so prominent in contemporary times.

Davide Ponzini

process has made the widespread circulation of advanced architectural solutions and technologies possible, but it has also had negative environmental effects and led to increasing cultural and urban homogenization. In my opinion, observing globalization in a generalized way does not allow us to fully understand the implications of the circulation of architectural solutions in specific areas nor does it work to improve their urban effects (Ponzini, 2020). On the contrary, following the transnational trajectories of specific actors over time between distinct places allows us to explain urban change and see the actors' role in it.

Permasteelisa offers a unique opportunity to interpret the historic and geographic trajectories of the advanced companies that compose the multinational Group and thus to explore these design technology providers' roles and contributions within different urban transformation processes. The Group has long been described as a "company of companies" as the parent firm ISA merged with and acquired a number of leading competitors over time (one can mention Permasteel, Scheldebouw B.V., and Josef Gartner GmbH) becoming today's Permasteelisa Group. The "history of histories" of the Group's companies and branches and the composition of the diverse background and expertise that derived from it allows one to see different design technology providers together, trace their evolution in time and space, connect their completed projects and recurrent places, and finally explore their roles and contributions in changing the faces of contemporary cities. Permasteelisa Group's projects—over 1,500 curtain wall façade projects implemented in hundreds of cities—form a very significant pool, not only geographically and historically but also from a qualitative point of view. The interest in this actor lies in the capacity for experimentation and technical specialization that has contributed to the design and construction of the façade systems of many buildings that serve as icons and fabric for cities around the world. Permasteelisa's recurring partnerships—including Gehry Partners, Foster + Partners, Renzo Piano, Herzog & de Meuron, KPF, SOM, and others—have indisputable importance in contemporary architecture. Observing a technology provider of this level through an assemblage perspective questions authorship in architecture and the most typical narratives

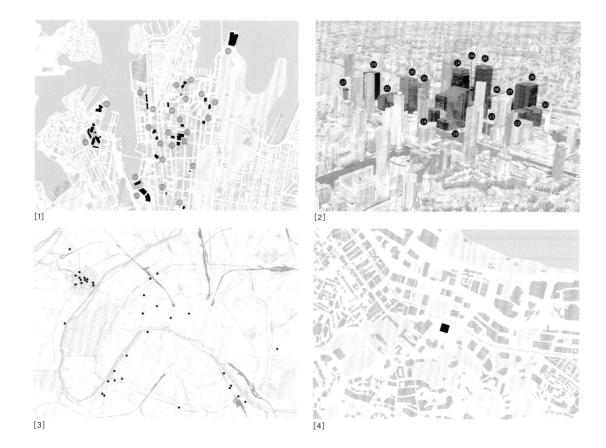

[1]

[2]

[3]

[4]

promoted by star architects. Permasteelisa techniques deal not only with the realizability of certain projects but also with the design process in general. It is important to note that the impact of the work of an actor like the Permasteelisa Group on the transformation of the face of contemporary cities does not depend only on the availability and circulation of innovative technologies but also on the compositional effect of their use in the same place, in the same city, by various transnational designers over time. Permasteelisa's work clearly affects a city's key buildings as well as numerous other important buildings that make up the fabric of central areas. These emerging buildings and their fabric often compose the imagery of that contemporary city—whether one likes these best-known faces or not. Finally, Permasteelisa's work traces a geography that does not only concern the West, but also and very intensely Asia, the Middle East, and Oceania. In this book, it was necessary to select a limited number of cities to test our hypothesis. Some cities have an indisputably top position in the global system, such as New York, London, Paris, Hong Kong, and Shanghai. Others have an important role in the global system due to their specialization, such as Frankfurt and Sydney. For each city, the clusters of Permasteelisa Group's projects will be highlighted and discussed with reference to the most characteristic urban areas. The cities considered are very different in terms of size and population. In the past fifty years, their demographic and economic dynamics differed significantly from one another. Basic data from the United Nations publications (2018) will be reported to give the reader a sense, for each city, of the urban population scale and change over time. The current city product per capita (Statista, 2022) will be shown for each city. The variety of places selected allows us to see different situations and to explore our hypothesis in an articulated way.

The book then delves into twelve individual buildings—some are located in the seven cities selected while others are not—that allow for further reflections. These buildings influence not only the face of their own city but also others through links that will be evident in considering the technologies and actors who have contributed to assembling them. We also considered individual projects prior to the historical period of reference to show how the trajectory of Permasteelisa derives from many stories of technology providers who have contributed to the formation and growth of the Group over time, like Permasteel, Gartner, and Scheldebouw. As we know, Permasteelisa has been a "company of companies," and today we can consider their long-term trajectories in a unified way.

The faces of this book

In addition to this introduction, the book is structured in five chapters. The first two are historical insights, while the following two are geographic insights at different scales. The first chapter "Contemporary architecture to the test of the history of constructors" by Paolo Scrivano develops an unprecedented perspective on the history of architecture. In fact, Permasteelisa's works make it possible to observe several masterpieces of contemporary architecture from the point of view of the same group of technology providers and not from the typical point of view of architectural design firms. The second chapter by Mario Carpo delves into a specific technology and shows its rise, diffusion, and impact on the design of the façades of iconic buildings in various cities around the world. The third chapter that I authored shows various urban geographies that emerge from the transnational analysis of Permasteelisa's trajectories and works discussed in this book. The fourth chapter "Networks of architectural production: Behind the façade of Hamburg's Elbphilharmonie" by Johannes Dreher and Joachim Thiel, illustrates how the façade of a complex project is the result of a network of expertise and production on a regional and international scale. Some innovations from this particular assemblage later influenced iconic projects in other cities. Finally, in the fifth chapter, Marco Antonio Minozzo Gabriel reports the historical and geographical analysis of Permasteelisa's work through the documentation that has supported our investigation and we hope will be useful for further research. This book explores a new perspective concerning the contribution of a technology provider to the evolution of cities and presents methods for articulating it in time and space. Under this perspective, there are multiple questions that our limited work cannot answer.

First of all, a more radical reflection on the authorship of architectural and urban projects would make it possible to "reframe" the history of architecture and the city from this perspective, not just a technological one but one that relates the socio-material assemblage of notable buildings and central places. Permasteelisa's work historically develops not only along architecture's disciplinary discourse but also along urban planning and environmental discourses. A more in-depth study of the sustainability of specific typologies (prominently that of the high-rise tower) and of the aggregate effects at different scales on the built environment seems urgent today. I am convinced that Permasteelisa's work deserves more attention and a systematic mapping of all the projects carried out in its fifty years of history. Collecting and analyzing the complete data requires a much greater research effort beyond the scope of this book. It would lead to formulating and answering numerous research questions on transnational urbanism and architecture in an innovative way. As an example, projects could be investigated in places that do not characterize the identity of cities, such as the so-called non-places (e.g. airports and stations) or projects in non-urban places. Furthermore, investigating the relationships and forms of collaboration between the Permasteelisa Group and prominent design firms would allow one to deepen the analysis of the design process, the mutual influence between experts, and how they adapt to specific urban conditions. This applies to other technology providers, developers, and main contractors as well.

I think that further historical, urban planning, architectural, and sociological research would provide important feedback to the Group itself, its strategies, and its work in the coming decades. In this sense, further research is needed, benefiting Permasteelisa not only by having a greater awareness of its own work but also by recognizing and improving its urban contributions. A different perception of the role of design technology providers in affecting cities and in their history, as well as sustainability matters, entails important development opportunities for the future, but also great responsibilities.

MAP OF THE CITIES SELECTED FOR ANALYSIS

The exploration of the face of these seven cities allows for analysis and reflection regarding the role of Permasteelisa Group's companies. The cities cover a wide geographic scope and differ from one another from the historic, economic, and demographic points of view, considering the last fifty years especially.

LONDON

NEW YORK

PARIS

FRANKFURT

SHANGHAI

HONG KONG

SYDNEY

Lloyd's Building
LONDON, 1986

Elbphilharmonie
HAMBURG, 2016

The Shard
LONDON, 2012

Hearst Tower
NEW YORK, 2006

Guggenheim
Museum Bilbao
BILBAO, 1997

Glòries Tower
BARCELONA, 2005

SAS Royal Hotel
COPENHAGEN, 1960

Bank of China Tower
HONG KONG, 1990

M+
HONG KONG, 2021

UniCredit Tower
MILAN, 2012

HQ Building
ABU DHABI, 2010

Sydney Opera House
SYDNEY, 1973

INTERIOR OF 10 COLUMBUS CIRCLE
Close-up and interior photographs may include design and technological details. The selection in this book is somewhat different as it intends to reconnect those buildings with their urban context, just as the whole book does for the work of design technology providers.

PAGE 24
ONE57 TOWER

New York

USA

1970
URBAN POPULATION*

16.19 M

*New York-Newark urban agglomeration

2020
URBAN POPULATION*

18.80 M

**CITY PRODUCT
PER CAPITA (US$)**

71,312

0   1,000   2,000 m

0   2,500   5,000 ft

Lower Manhattan

A selection of the projects completed by the Permasteelisa Group, name of the main architecture firm, and year of completion.

01	Goldman Sachs Headquarters	*Pei Cobb Freed & Partners*	2010
02	111 Murray Street	*Kohn Pedersen Fox Associates (KPF)*	2019
03	World Financial Center, Glass Pavilion at The Winter Garden	*Pelli Clarke Pelli Architects*	1988
04	7 World Trade Center	*Skidmore, Owings & Merrill (SOM)*	2006
05	One World Trade Center (podium)	*Skidmore, Owings & Merrill (SOM)*	2014
06	The Ronald O. Perelman Performing Arts Center	*REX*	2022

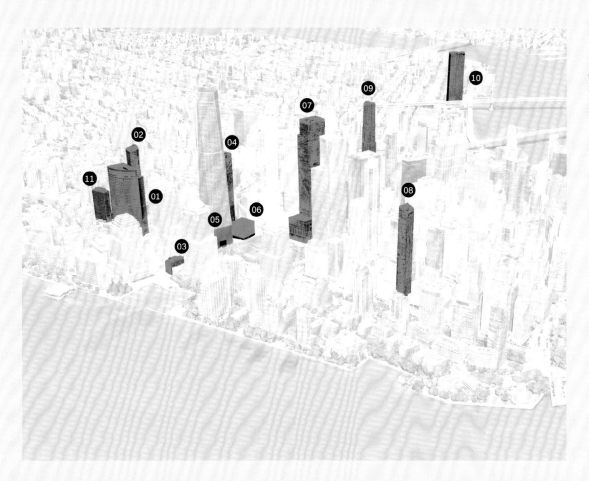

07	3 World Trade Center (Marriott World Trade Center)	*Rogers Stirk Harbour + Partners*	2018
08	50 West Street	*Jahn*	2017
09	Eight Spruce Street (New York by Gehry; Beekman Tower)	*Gehry Partners*	2011
10	One Manhattan Square	*Adamson Associates*	2019
11	200 Chambers Street	*Cosentini Associates*	2007

New York is one of the most important world capitals for business, innovation, and culture. It has a vast set of specialized functions and is highly connected to its region, country, and most world capitals. It has long been a testing ground for modern architectural and urban planning innovation, particularly when it comes to high-rise buildings and business districts. Nevertheless, the vast majority of the city's buildings are generic and hardly recognizable when isolated from the skyline image. Since the 2000s, a new wave of innovative projects altered the character of key areas such as Lower Manhattan and Midtown. The redevelopment of the World Trade Center site and the Eight Spruce Street skyscraper by Frank Gehry changed perceptions of the downtown. The Midtown area near Central Park has gradually evolved toward higher and higher buildings with the construction not only of 10 Columbus Circle by SOM and the Hearst Corporation headquarters by Norman Foster, but also of supertalls such as One57 by Christian de Portzamparc. World-class interventions and substantial urban regeneration have also transformed other places, including the Meatpacking District and the High Line Elevated Park development that now attracts millions of visitors every year. Important buildings such as the InterActiveCorp Building by Frank Gehry and the new Whitney Museum by Renzo Piano reinforced the ongoing transformation and its international visibility. Permasteelisa Group's contribution was key to all these highly visible projects. While the Group started working with higher intensity in the USA only at the end of the 1990s, New York City alone has seen more than sixty projects completed since then.

PREVIOUS PAGES
VIEW OF DOWNTOWN MANHATTAN

LEFT
7 WORLD TRADE CENTER

Midtown Manhattan

A selection of the projects completed by the Permasteelisa Group, name of the main architecture firm, and year of completion.

01	Deutsche Bank Center (10 Columbus Circle)	*Skidmore, Owings & Merrill (SOM)*	2004
02	Hearst Tower	*Foster + Partners*	2006
03	Central Park Tower	*Adrian Smith + Gordon Gill Architecture*	2022
04	Courtyard New York Manhattan (1717 Broadway)	*Nobutaka Ashihara Architect*	2013
05	One57 (Carnegie 57)	*Christian de Portzamparc*	2014
06	555 10th Avenue	*SLCE Architects*	2016
07	Intercontinental New York Times Square	*Gensler*	2010
08	Museum of Modern Art MoMA (renovation)	*Yoshio Taniguchi*	2005
09	The Westin New York at Times Square	*Arquitectonica*	2002
10	Eleven Times Square	*FXFOWLE*	2011
11	Times Square Tower	*Skidmore, Owings & Merrill (SOM)*	2004

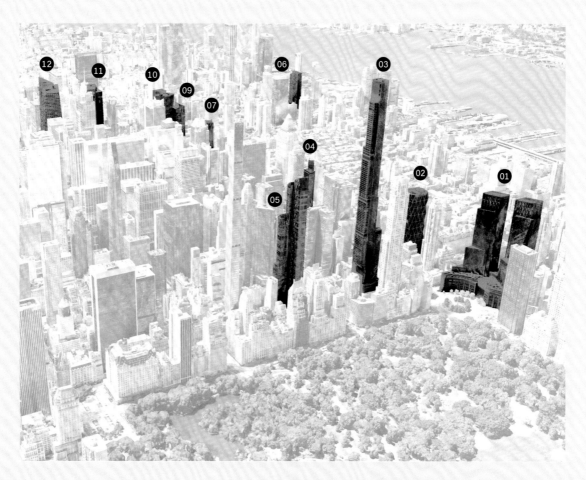

12	One Bryant Park (Bank of America Tower)	COOKFOX Architects	2009
13	50 West 47th Street (International Gem Tower)	Skidmore, Owings & Merrill (SOM)	2012
14	510 Madison Avenue	SLCE Architects	2010
15	550 Madison (canopy)	Snøhetta	2022
16	130 East 59th Street	Swanke Hayden Connell Architects	2007
17	425 Park Avenue	Foster + Partners	2021
18	360 Madison Avenue	Jaros, Baum & Bolles	2002
19	560 Lexington Avenue	Skidmore, Owings & Merrill (SOM)	2015
20	Selene (100 East 53rd Street)	Foster + Partners	2018
21	The Centrale (138 East 50th Street)	Pelli Clarke Pelli Architects	2021
22	One Vanderbilt	Kohn Pedersen Fox Associates (KPF)	2021

VIEW OF DOWNTOWN MANHATTAN AND THE BROOKLYN BRIDGE

Chapter 1

Contemporary architecture to the test of the history of constructors

Paolo Scrivano

Centered on singular biographies, outstanding architectures, or big events, the prevailing narratives of architectural history seldom consider the involvement of other actors in the processes leading to the realization of built artifacts. While the role played by clients has received some attention in the past, little reflection seems to have been given to the part that contractors, construction companies, and technology providers normally have in the design and building activities.

The history of the Permasteelisa Group, as derived from both internal growth and the amalgamation of different preexisting industrial realities, challenges these deeply rooted historiographical views. Permasteelisa's portfolio overlaps with many other narratives covering the last seven decades of the history of architecture. However, the company's involvement in these historical narratives imposes a reassessment of the responsibilities for the aesthetic, functional, and technological decisions behind the works that are presented in them as well.

This essay intends to use the case of Permasteelisa to reexamine the relationship between the different actors that participate in the design process. By placing "high-profile" buildings in a wider epistemological context, the essay aims to lay the ground for a new historiographical approach that looks at architecture not merely as the result of select individual choices, but as an assemblage, a collective and more complex endeavor involving a multiplicity of actors.

TAIPEI 101, TAIPEI
A powerful illustration of the so-called "race toward the sky" that marked the architectural and engineering scene of the last three decades, Taipei 101 was the world's tallest building from its opening in 2004 until 2009, when its primacy was overcome by Dubai's Burj Khalifa.

Architects, clients, contractors, design expertise: A historiographical overview

The history of architecture is dominated by narratives where the involvement of actors other than architects is seldom considered. In most historical accounts of modern and contemporary architecture, the processes leading to the realization of built artifacts are typically centered on singular biographies, by and large of male individuals, or on outstanding architectures and big events. Those who bring the buildings about, from the contractors to the workforce, are rarely included in this picture, and even less so those who use them. Indeed, this "narrative of the individual" has a long lineage, rooted as it is in a well-established tradition of histories of "lives of great artists," dating back in the West to Renaissance time (Scrivano, 2012). However, it is surprising how this storyline has managed to survive for so long, in spite of the growing complexity of today's design and construction practices: it would be safe to say that it has even gained further currency in the current media-dominated society, one where "Master builders" are often presented as public heroes (Foster, 2002, 27–42). When architectural historians' attention has not been exclusively addressed to architects, or to any professional charged with the task of conceiving and designing a building, the focus has been placed on clients. Starting from the pioneering works of the early 1980s on Le Corbusier and his clients, both private and institutional, a significant scholarship on this subject has developed over the years (Croset, 1980; Maniaque, 2005). By and large, though, this interest in the relations linking architects and their clientele replicates a historiographical approach homed in on the interactions between individuals, with its implicit conceptual corollary: that little reflection pinpoints the part that contrac-

tors, construction companies, and technology providers normally have in the design and building activities. For this reason, it is perhaps foreseeable that existing research on contractors, construction companies, but also on building promoters, and real estate developers, is often dominated by specialists in the history of economy (Fohlen, 1978; Barjot, 1996): in this scholarship, no doubt solid and convincing, considerations on the role played by architects are for the most part absent. Researchers in urban studies have delved into the profiles of real estate developers, including sometimes powerful institutional "power brokers" (Fainstein, 1994; Ballon and Jackson, 2007), but just a few studies have given a precise account of the part assigned to architects in distinct design processes, as in the case of the collaboration between Richard Roth, Walter Gropius, and Pietro Belluschi, on the one hand, and builder and real estate developers and structural engineers, on the other, in materializing the Pan Am Building in New York (Clausen, 2005). Connections between design and execution are neglected altogether: social engagement often emerges as a defining factor, whether under the form of a political commitment, such as in the foundation of building cooperatives (Gagès, 1989), or of specialization in specific sectors, such as state-funded social housing (Jambard, 2008). Scholarship originating from the field of architectural history has rather emphasized the connection between architecture and engineering, following ideological agendas meant to promote select movements and tendencies, such as modernism (Drexler, 1964). Recently, attention has been brought to large design and building conglomerates, such as Maire Tecnimont (the former FIAT Engineering and Servizio Costruzioni FIAT), whose identities lie between the two disciplines (Comba, 2011). National perspectives persist and remain central (Dobbels, 2021).

Still missing within this panorama are analyses on the variety of actors that have dominated the postwar building scene and still command it: from the Società Generale Immobiliare (or SGI), an Italian building promoter with close ties to the Vatican known also for the construction of the Torre Velasca in Milan (1955–57) and for the collaboration with architect Luigi Moretti in the realization of the Tour de la Bourse in Montréal (1960–65) and the Watergate complex in Washington, D.C. (1962–71) (Spina, 2022); to Bouygues and Dumez in France, Skansa in Sweden (whose portfolio includes, among others, Norman Foster and Ove Arup's Swiss Re in London), or real estate developers like China's Vanke, Australia's Lendlease, and the Texas-headquartered Hines (the last two partners of the Permasteelisa Group in a number of construction endeavors). Historians seem to be daunted by the task of looking at the history of architecture through the lens of the construction and technology providers' roles, while they should instead grasp not only the importance of their involvement but also the intrinsic fascination of considering the design process in a more complex way. The Petronas Towers in Kuala Lampur, Malaysia (1994–2001), provide a case in point. While the design was carried out by a management team from

TORRE VELASCA, MILAN
Designed by the Milanese BBPR firm, the Torre Velasca responded to the question of inserting a high-rise into a historically layered city fabric. Its visual dialogue with existing symbols of Milan, such as the Duomo and the Castello Sforzesco, made it a world-recognized icon.

PETRONAS TOWERS, KUALA LUMPUR
A truly transnational operation in terms of both design and construction, the Petronas Towers were meant to celebrate Malaysia's newly acquired status of international economic player, thanks to the country's expansive development in the oil extraction business.

Paolo Scrivano

Kuala Lumpur City Centre Berhad (KLCCB) and by Cesar Pelli and Associates in New York, the works were awarded to two consortia, one led by Hazama Ando Corporation, one of Japan's biggest building companies, and including another Japanese enterprise, Mitsubishi, and the other led by South Korean conglomerate Samsung Engineering and Construction (*Sculpting the Sky: Petronas Twin Towers*, KLCC, 1998). Without a doubt, the story of the towers' project execution elucidates the intricated practices behind a building's construction in a more convincing way than any narrative centered on engineering performance or technological prowess.

GUGGENHEIM MUSEUM BILBAO, BILBAO

The structure of Frank Gehry's Guggenheim Museum Bilbao results from the use of new systems of design and calculation and from the employ of materials that had previously found little application in the building industry. It denotes the discrepancy between representation and execution that might still exist in particularly innovative projects (like the Walt Disney Concert Hall, also by Gehry).

The history of contemporary architecture vis à vis assemblages of design and technological and construction expertise

Hardly any architecture, in any moment in history, has been the outcome of a single individual's work; nor has it been entirely unaffected by the presence of successive generations of users. Buildings are neither the direct translation of one's ideas nor frozen in time. The close interlacement of architectural design, building engineering, and construction, which characterizes most contemporary architectures, entails a more intricate understanding of the historical and cultural contexts within which they originate since what can be called "assemblages" of design occur in specific geographical locations and chronological settings (Farías and Bender, 2010). For example, both Frank Gehry's Walt Disney Concert Hall in Los Angeles (appointment 1987–completion 2003) and the Guggenheim Museum in Bilbao (1991–97), two of the most iconic buildings of Permasteelisa's portfolio, owe their fame to their aesthetic appearance, the result of the architects' use of new systems of design and calculation, but also of the employ of materials such as aluminum and titanium that became available after the fall of Europe's Communist Bloc in the early 1990s and the subsequent collapse of its armament industry. What passes often unnoticed is the detachment that exists in these two works between the formal sophistication of the external coating and the sheer simplicity of the supporting structure.

This disconnection is by no means novel in the history of architecture, as the case of Erich Mendelsohn's Einstein Tower, built in Potsdam between 1919 and 1921, proves. Conceived to be realized in ferroconcrete, it was then completed by relying on traditional brick masonry construction, owing to the complexity of the required formworks and

Contemporary architecture to the test of the history of constructors

the scarcity of steel in post–World War I Germany: the outside curvilinear surfaces, which mimicked the plastic effect of concrete poured into rounded molds, were obtained by simply covering the walls of the building's upper part with stucco (James, 1997, 28–34). In Mendelsohn's instance, the conversion into architectural forms of a cultural and aesthetic statement, one that associated a technological system to an idea of modernity, collided with a reality that limited the designers' and builders' range of action. In Gehry's case, it was the distance between available  techniques of representation and actual capabilities of the construction sector that required a "fix" destined to remain hidden behind the shiny surfaces of the aluminum and titanium panels. Coming to terms with the realization that architectural history cannot be reduced to a history of architects, of "master builders" almost removed from the context in which they "materially" conduct their profession, prompts more than one reflection on the epistemological nature of the discipline. First and foremost, it touches on still-unaddressed questions of authorship; then it forces a reconsideration of existing chronologies and genealogies; finally, it indicates the need for a reassessment of all the elements (factual, cultural, intellectual) that constitute the "history" of a given work of architecture. The involvement of the Permasteelisa Group, as the amalgamation of several preexisting industrial realities, in almost seven decades of architectural history thus challenges deeply rooted and firmly established historiographical views: if the overlapping of the Group's portfolio with the current narratives of the history of contemporary architecture is apparent, it is even more evident that the responsibility for the aesthetic, functional and technological decisions that characterize the works presented in these outlines needs to undergo a thorough reexamination.

Many architectures that form the history of the Permasteelisa Group could be taken as examples. Arne Jacobsen's SAS Hotel in Copenhagen (1956–60) provided as much of an opportunity for experimentation in curtain wall technique as it set a standard for Europe's postwar modernist multistory buildings (Hitchcock, 1962); Egon Eiermann and Paul Schneider–Esleben's Mannesmann Office Building in Düsseldorf (1954–58) marked the belated coming to the fore of the "Neues Bauen" in Germany (Frank, 1993); Jørn Utzon's Sydney Opera House (1958–73) supplied a city with a landmark destined to become a recognized symbol as well as it gave the start to a construction undertaking indicated as a prime instance of deprovincialization of an entire (and outdated) building sector (Murray, 2004).

These considerations can be extended to works completed in the last three decades. Chu-yuan Lee and Chung-ping Wang's Taipei 101, in Taipei, Taiwan (1999–2004), engaged in an international "race toward the sky" that briefly placed it at the top of the list of the tallest buildings in the world (until 2009, when it was surpassed by Adrian Smith and Skidmore, Owings & Merrill's Burj Khalifa in Dubai). With its 1,667 feet of height and 101 floors, together with its allusion to the shape of a bamboo culm, this

LEFT
SYDNEY OPERA HOUSE, SYDNEY
The Opera House shows Jørn Utzon's attempt to combine different stylistic and cultural references. Realized thanks to the involvement of Ove Arup and Partners' engineering firm, it has become the icon of Sydney. The construction of the Opera House marked the starting point of a process of deprovincialization of Australia's outdated building sector.

SAS ROYAL HOTEL, COPENHAGEN
Credited as one of the prime examples of "European skyscrapers" of the postwar years, the SAS Royal Hotel provided an opportunity for experimentation in curtain wall technique.

skyscraper transformed the skyline of Taipei, supplying the city with a recognizable icon in a sort of extravagant "Bilbao effect" transposed to the Far East (Ockman, 2004). The same spectacularism of design practices also characterizes Jacques Herzog and Pierre de Meuron's Elbphilharmonie in Hamburg (2001–16) (Balke, Reuber, and Wood, 2018). Even more, with its center status within a network of expertise and production, the Elbphilharmonie highlights the importance of the circulation of technical knowledge, a question that has emerged as central to current research in the fields of architecture, urban design, and urbanism: as such, Herzog & de Meuron's building represents an exceptional case in point for a transnational approach to the study of architectural history (Scrivano, 2009; Ponzini, 2020).

The same transnational approach that is indispensable for any historical investigation into Permasteelisa Group's participation in the realization of these and other buildings. In this brief listing of Permasteelisa's works, Daniel Libeskind's extension of the Royal Ontario Museum in Toronto (2001–07) deserves a particular mention. Now called Michael Lee-Chin Crystal extension, this artifact reveals how technological and aesthetic solutions can be combined to gain center stage in public discourses, most probably contingent on fundraising goals. Moreover, with its close resemblance to the Military History Museum in Dresden (2001–11), another project by Libeskind, the museum in Toronto proves how "families" of buildings sharing similar aesthetic and technological solutions participate in the construction of public imaginaries and professional identities. Therefore, rewriting the narratives of contemporary architectural history implies considering these and other works with a different methodological an epistemological gaze.

EXTENSION OF THE ROYAL ONTARIO MUSEUM, TORONTO
The conception and construction of the Royal Ontario Museum's new extension reflected the climate of the city of Toronto at the beginning of the twenty-first century, where several institutions competed over providing the city with new and compelling cultural landmarks.

Paolo Scrivano

Conclusions: The history of a technology provider in the wider context of history

So far, investigations into the contribution of design and technology service providers in giving shape and visual significance to individual buildings have been rare in number and limited in scope. This scarcity has also led to overlooking the role they have played in defining the features of contemporary cities. This is rather striking since American architectural historian Henry-Russell Hitchcock had, in the mid-1950s, pointed at urban façades in South American cities as evidence of deep economic, societal, and cultural transformations: Hitchcock argued that one of the most remarkable characteristics of Latin American architecture was not only its coherence with the canons of prewar modernism, featuring simple volumes and using "modern" materials such as reinforced concrete, steel, and glass, but also the capacity to contribute to the renovation of urban environments (Hitchcock, 1955). The history of Permasteelisa as the unification of the histories of the companies that form today's Group would deserve a closer analysis, one that perhaps would be better written by industry historians. But a discussion from the point of view of the architectural historian historicizing the buildings in whose realization the Permasteelisa Group has been involved allows for a reexamination of the relationship among the different actors that participate in the design and building process, for questioning current notions of authorship, for a new understanding of how architecture engages in public discourses (Jannière and Scrivano, 2020).

By placing these "high-profile" works in a wider epistemological context, it might become possible to lay the groundwork for a renewed historiographical approach that looks at architecture not merely as the result of select individual choices but as a collective and more complex endeavor marked by a transnational web of professional and technological trajectories.

EXTENSION OF THE ROYAL ONTARIO MUSEUM, TORONTO
While the intricated volumes of the new extension produced the anticipated visual impact, they also imposed an organization of the internal spaces that conflicts with the image of "transparency" used to promote the building at the time of the fundraising campaign.

PAGE 48
VIEW OF CANARY WHARF

London
UK

1970
URBAN POPULATION

7.51 M

2020
URBAN POPULATION

9.30 M

CITY PRODUCT
PER CAPITA (US$)

45,611

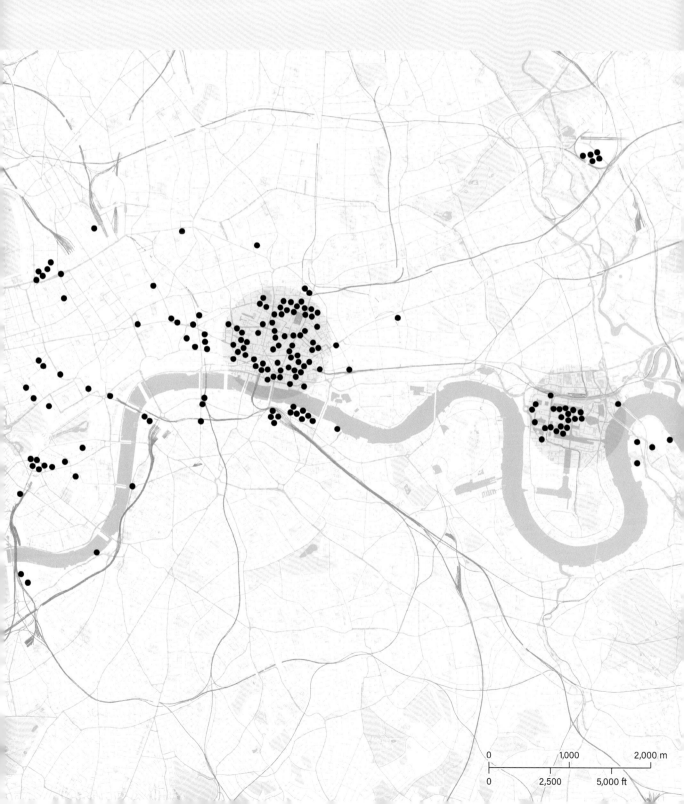

City of London

A selection of the projects completed by
the Permasteelisa Group, name of the main architecture firm,
and year of completion.

01	One Bartholomew	*Sheppard Robson*	2018
02	One London Wall	*Foster + Partners*	2003
03	Shelley House	*Sheppard Robson*	1998
04	150 Cheapside	*Michael Aukett Architects*	2009
05	10 Gresham Street	*Foster + Partners*	2003
06	20 Gresham Street	*Kohn Pedersen Fox Associates (KPF)*	2008
07	One Wood Street	*Fletcher Priest Architects*	2007
08	One New Change	*Ateliers Jean Nouvel*	2010
09	Bow Bells House	*David Walker Architects*	2008
10	4 Cannon Street	*PLP Architecture*	2019
11	60 Queen Victoria Street	*Foggo Associates*	1999
12	Bloomberg Headquarters	*Foster + Partners*	2017
13	The Walbrook Building	*Foster + Partners*	2009
14	Cannon Place	*Foggo Associates*	2011

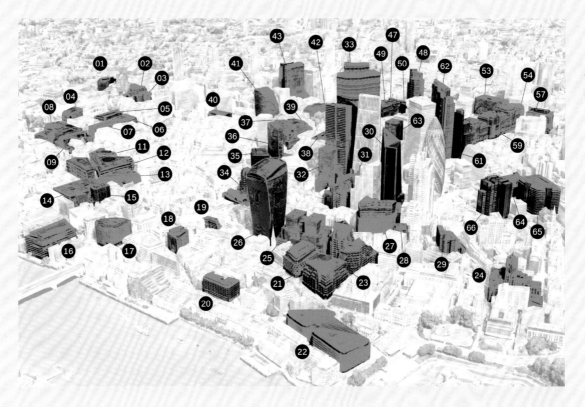

15	Bush Lane House	*Arup*	1976
16	Riverbank House	*David Walker Architects*	2010
17	33 Central (33 King William Street)	*John Robertson Architects*	2017
18	The Monument Building (The Monument Estate)	*Make*	2016
19	50-54 Gracechurch Street (renovation)	*EPR Architects*	1981
20	Watermark Place	*Fletcher Priest Architects*	2009
21	Plantation Place South	*Arup*	2004
22	Tower Place	*Foster + Partners*	2002
23	1-3 Minster Court	*GMW Architects*	1991
24	One America Square	*RHWL Architects*	1990
25	Plantation Place	*Arup*	2004
26	20 Fenchurch Street	*Rafael Viñoly Architects*	2014
27	One Fen Court (10 Fenchurch Avenue)	*Eric Parry Architects*	2018
28	AIG Building (58 Fenchurch Street)	*Kohn Pedersen Fox Associates (KPF)*	2002
29	71 Fenchurch (Lloyd's Register of Shipping)	*Rogers Stirk Harbour + Partners*	2000
30	52 Lime Street	*Kohn Pedersen Fox Associates (KPF)*	2020
31	Lloyd's Building	*Rogers Stirk Harbour + Partners*	1986
32	4 Bishopsgate	*GMW Architects*	1981
33	22 Bishopsgate	*PLP Architecture*	2020
34	54 Lombard Street	*GMW Architects*	1993

35	60 Threadneedle Street	*Eric Parry Architects*	2009
36	125 Old Broad Street (renovation and extension)	*GMW Architects*	2008
37	Drapers Gardens	*Foggo Associates*	2009
38	Winchester House	*Swanke Hayden Connell Architects*	1999
39	60 London Wall	*EPR Architects*	2020
40	One Basinghall Avenue	*Bennetts Associates*	2007
41	Moor House	*Foster + Partners*	2004
42	Lutyens House (renovation)	*Nimmo and Partners*	1989
43	Citypoint London	*Sheppard Robson*	2000
44	Milton Court	*David Walker Architects*	2013
45	Milton Gate	*Denys Lasdun, Peter Softley & Partners*	1989
46	The Helicon (Finsbury Pavement)	*Sheppard Robson*	1996
47	2 Finsbury Avenue	*Arup*	1988
48	One Crown Place	*Kohn Pedersen Fox Associates (KPF)*	2021
49	1 Finsbury Avenue	*Arup*	1984
50	3 Finsbury Avenue	*Arup*	1986

51	Bavaria House (13-14 Appold Street)	Covell Matthews Wheatley Architects	1988
52	Broadgate Phase 11 Westwing	Skidmore, Owings & Merrill (SOM)	1990
53	Broadgate Exchange House (10 Exchange Square)	Skidmore, Owings & Merrill (SOM)	1990
54	199 Bishopsgate (EC2; Broadgate Phase 14)	Skidmore, Owings & Merrill (SOM)	1991
55	1 Appold Street (Broadgate Phase 5)	Skidmore, Owings & Merrill (SOM)	1988
56	288 Bishopsgate	Foggo Associates	2000
57	280 Bishopsgate	Foggo Associates	2001
58	1 Bishops Square	Foster + Partners	2004
59	136-175 Bishopsgate (Broadgate Phases 6-8)	Skidmore, Owings & Merrill (SOM)	1989
60	NIDO Spitalfields	tp bennett	2010
61	ONE Bishopsgate Plaza (150 Bishopsgate)	PLP Architecture	2021
62	Salesforce Tower (110 Bishopsgate)	Kohn Pedersen Fox Associates (KPF)	2012
63	99 Bishopsgate	GMW Architects	1994
64	Five Acre Square	cfp architects	1991
65	St. Botolphs Building	Grimshaw Architects	2010
66	One Creechurch Place	Sheppard Robson	2016

London was the thriving heart of a vast empire for centuries. After World War II, it evolved into a central node for international networks of trade, finance, and advanced services, as well as remaining a place of political power and cultural influence. The contemporary city fabric and individual iconic buildings reflect this. In the twentieth century, few new buildings in the city center stood out, one exception being the Lloyd's Building designed by Richard Rogers. One area visibly exempt to height limitations in London was Canary Wharf, the new business district that emerged in the 1990s on the site of the former docklands. The Permasteelisa Group supported international firms such as Pelli Clarke Pelli Architects, Foster + Partners, HOK, KPF, and SOM in implementing more than twenty buildings, shaping the exteriors of the entire area. Since the 2000s, the local government has allowed high-rise developments in other areas, such as the City of London. Once more, the Group's work contributed to realizing key buildings and the new urban fabric, with projects like the 20 Fenchurch Street building designed by Rafael Viñoly and the Bloomberg Headquarters by Foster + Partners. In the 2010s, the completion of the Shard building, designed by Renzo Piano Building Workshop, added an iconic landmark to Southwark and changed its neighborhood's functional balance and accessibility through the London Bridge station. The Group did not only partner with prominent international architects but also with repeat clients, like Mace, Lendlease, Skanska, ISG, SRM, Balfour Beatty, and other main contractors. The Group has contributed to shaping London's contemporary face with more than 200 projects completed by different Permasteelisa companies since the 1980s.

Canary Wharf

A selection of the projects completed by the Permasteelisa Group, name of the main architecture firm, and year of completion.

1	17 Columbus Courtyard (B4)	*Gensler*	1999
2	20 Columbus Courtyard (B5)	*Skidmore, Owings & Merrill (SOM)*	1999
3	No. 1 West India Quay	*HOK*	2004
4	25 North Colonnade (FC3)	*John McAslan + Partners*	1991
5	Bank of America (5 Canada Square)	*Skidmore, Owings & Merrill (SOM)*	2002
6	HSBC UK Headquarters (8 Canada Square)	*Foster + Partners*	2002
7	KPMG European Headquarters (15 Canada Square)	*Kohn Pedersen Fox Associates (KPF)*	2011
8	30 North Colonnade (DS3 East)	*Kohn Pedersen Fox Associates (KPF)*	2010
9	One Churchill Place (BP1)	*HOK*	2004
10	5 Churchill Place (BP2)	*HOK*	2009
11	Ontario Tower	*Skidmore, Owings & Merrill (SOM)*	2007

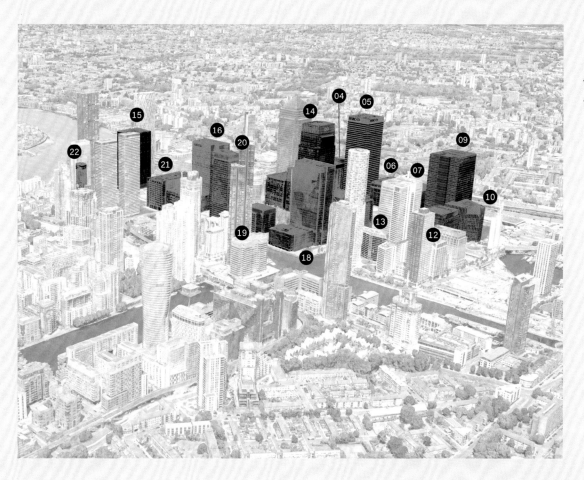

12	20 Churchill Place (BP3)	*Kohn Pedersen Fox Associates (KPF)*	2009
13	25 Canada Square (DS5)	*Pelli Clarke Pelli Architects*	2002
14	20 Canada Square (DS4)	*Skidmore, Owings & Merrill (SOM)*	2003
15	1 Bank Street	*Kohn Pedersen Fox Associates (KPF)*	2019
16	25 Bank Street (HQ2)	*Pelli Clarke Pelli Architects*	2003
17	East Winter Garden	*Pelli Clarke Pelli Architects*	2003
18	10 Upper Bank Street (HQ5)	*Kohn Pedersen Fox Associates (KPF)*	2003
19	50 Bank Street (HQ4)	*Pelli Clarke Pelli Architects*	2002
20	40 Bank Street (HQ3)	*Pelli Clarke Pelli Architects*	2003
21	20 Bank Street (HQ1)	*Skidmore, Owings & Merrill (SOM)*	2003
22	Novotel Canary Wharf	*Leach Rhodes Walker*	2016

THE CITY OF LONDON SEEN FROM SAINT PAUL'S CATHEDRAL

Chapter 2

Digital mass-customization and the rise of the nonstandard architectural envelope

Mario Carpo

The modernist curtain wall was a product and symbol
of the technical logic of industrial mass production.
Mechanical technologies achieve economies of scale through
the identical replication of standardized components.
Using today's digital technologies of design and fabrication,
however, mass-produced components can be made all different,
in theory, at no additional cost ("digital mass-customization"),
and complex geometries, and irregular (non-geometrical)
forms are often seen, to this day, as the specific style
of a new architecture of the digital age.
This chapter focuses on the first iconic nonstandard
envelopes designed in 1990s by architect Frank Gehry,
which were built thanks to technology provided by French
software (and aircraft) maker Dassault and Italian curtain
wall specialist Permasteelisa.

High modernism times: Mass-production and curtain walls

WALT DISNEY CONCERT HALL, LOS ANGELES
The design and construction of this project ran almost parallel to the Guggenheim Museum Bilbao (see pages 176–181). In both projects Frank Gehry's office used technology by the Permasteelisa Group.

At some point in the early 1920s an ambitious young watchmaker, recently arrived in Paris from his native Swiss Jura (and soon to become famous under the *nom de plume* Le Corbusier) had an epiphany. The first automobiles were expensive, remarked young Le Corbusier, because each car was custom-made and made to order by specialized artisans, like a bespoke suit. Then Henry Ford started to mass-produce identical cars in factories, and made cars cheaper; so cheap that his own assembly-line workers could afford to buy the cars they made. Hence Le Corbusier's idea: Why should we not make buildings in the same way as Ford made cars? Housing is expensive because buildings are hand-made and made to order, mostly on-site. If we could mass-produce standardized buildings in the modern, industrial way, we would make them cheaper—just like cars became cheaper when they started being factory-made. One hundred years later we can tell, with a reasonable amount of confidence, that the argument was sound. However, when Le Corbusier started to actually build some buildings, he soon realized that prefabricating houses in a factory was (as it still is) a very tall order. Hence Le Corbusier looked for, and found, a middle ground: while the core of the building, its reinforced concrete structure, had to be made on site in the traditional, artisanal way (never mind that reinforced concrete itself was then a very new material), the most visible part of the building, its envelope, could indeed be factory-made. Factories of the time could in theory already mass-produce glass and steel windows, just as they mass-produced automobile windscreens and doors. As it happens, Le Corbusier's first curtain walls were almost entirely made by hand, being as they were one-off, small-size experiments; but Le Corbusier designed them to look as he thought they would look if they had been mass-produced in huge factories churning out millions of identical pieces a day. It took some time—probably longer than Le Corbusier had envisaged—but after the war, particularly in America, the industrial curtain wall did in fact become a ubiquitous feature of modern architecture. Mies van der Rohe translated its technical logic into a work of art: even if each component of the façades of the Seagram Building (1954–58) was custom-designed, each was replicated identically thousands of times; the Seagram was one of the most expensive buildings ever built, but at the same time a monument to the economics of industrial mass-production, and a celebration of the iron law of

SWISS PAVILION, PARIS
The Swiss Pavilion was designed by Le Corbusier and completed (1930–33) at the Cité Internationale Universitaire in Paris. It has become a reference for modernist architecture.

mechanical modernity: when things are made in a factory, the more identical copies we make, the cheaper each copy will be. That was the spirit of what today we call "high modernism": that brief but pervasive spell of socio-technical optimism, between the end of World War II and, roughly, the assassination of US president John F. Kennedy, when a new consumer culture enthusiastically endorsed industrial standards, and standards were universally seen as the image and icon of modernity and progress, and the promise of better times to come.

That optimism, however, did not last. Already in the 1960s some started to find industrial standards a bit boring (Robert Venturi, famously, in 1966); soon thereafter a new quest for visual variations coalesced around the tenets of architectural postmodernism. Yet industrial curtain walls kept being made pretty much the same, as not much had changed in the technology underpinning them. Postmodernist curtain walls were often deeply tinted or mirror-like, and vilipended by all and sundry for a number of different reasons (including, as of the early 1970s, due to new but rising concerns with energy savings and thermal performance). Then, in the early 1990s, a new technology emerged that revolutionized the way architectural envelopes are made and the way they look.

From mechanical mass-production to digital mass-customization

Computer-based CAD-CAM (Computer-Aided Design and Computer-Aided Manufacturing) have already upended the design and fabrication of almost everything—including the design and fabrication of architectural panels, out of which building envelopes are made. Here a brief technical digression is warranted. While most mechanical making needs casts, dies, stamps, or molds—mechanical matrixes of which the cost must be amortized by repeated use—digital fabrication (whether by milling, 3D printing, or robotic assembly) is for the most part not matrix-based. In the absence of a reusable matrix, making more identical replications of the same model will not save either time or labor and, conversely, variations in a digital design-to-manufacturing workflow do not entail supplemental costs. This mode of production is called "digital mass-customization." Unlike mechanical mass-production, digital mass-customization does not need to scale up to break even: the unit cost of a digitally fabricated panel is the same no matter how many we make; a factory could make one million identical copies of the same panel, or one million different panels (within the same production chain) at the same cost per panel. This is what economists call a "flat marginal cost" production, where economies of scale do not apply: in theory architectural envelopes could now be made of parts that are all different, or all the same, at the same cost; repeating the same panel everywhere will make many façades look the same but will not make any of them cheaper (Carpo, 2023). In practice, things do not yet really work that way. For one thing, panels must be assembled after being made, and the assembly of irregular panels is still a labor-intensive and expensive on-site operation, albeit now much facilitated by computational tools. In the foreseeable future, many of these on-site operations will be carried out by autonomous (AI-driven) robots. Nobody knows, however, when these technologies will be adopted by the construction industry (Zaera-Polo and Anderson, 2020). On the other hand, the impulse for the design of more and more convoluted architectural envelopes has emerged over the last thirty years from a range of cultural and formal motivations, which have often driven design intentions above and beyond deliverability.

Spline revolutions: Folding and streamlining

The rise of digital curviness is an exemplary case in point. As of the early 1990s a new generation of relatively cheap and user-friendly CAD software allowed the intuitive manipulation of a very special family of complex continuous curves, called "splines." Splines are streamlined, smooth curves used in shipbuilding to minimize the drag resulting from the movement of a boat's hull in water (hence the etymology of "streamlining," from "the line of the stream"). Artisan boat makers obtained splines through the mechanical bending and nailing of slats of wood. In the late 1950s and early 60s two French scientists, Pierre Bézier, an engineer by training, and mathematician Paul de Casteljau, working for the Renault and Citroën carmakers, respectively, discovered various methods for notating splines as mathematical functions, thus turning that centuries-old craft into a modern science. Bézier's math in particular, published in 1966, was the basis for UNISURF, the spline-modeling CAD software developed by Bézier's employer, Renault (as of 1968). UNISURF, in turn, was the basis of the CAD-CAM system developed internally by the Dassault aircraft company (then called Avions Marcel Dassault-Breguet Aviation) from 1977 to 1981, when it was renamed CATIA (Computer-Aided Three-Dimensional Interactive Application) to be marketed by the newly created subsidiary Dassault Systèmes. At the same time as de Casteljau's and Bézier's studies on free-form curves, similar research was carried out at MIT, Boeing, at the British Aircraft Corporation, and particularly by Carl de Boor at General Motors, which developed its own CAD-CAM system in the 1960s. In 1981 Boeing was among the first adopters (or perhaps the inventor) of NURBS, an acronym for Non Uniform, Rational Basis Splines, a new graphic format (and an international standard to this day) that merged Bézier's and de Casteljau's math with earlier studies by Princeton mathematician Isaac Jacob Schoenberg (Carpo, 2017). Bézier's, de Casteljeau's,

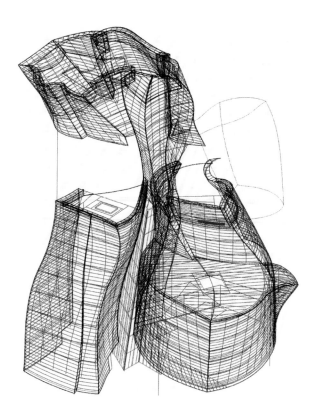

COMPUTER-
GENERATED
WIREFRAME OF
THE GUGGENHEIM
MUSEUM BILBAO
This project
required substantial
advancements in
computer-aided design
and manufacturing.

and Schoenberg's mathematical notations, when implemented by electronic computers, enormously simplified the design and fabrication of aerodynamic, or streamlined, shapes, and it is easy to see why this technology, discreetly but massively adopted by the aircraft, automobile, and shipbuilding industries as of the early 1980s, revolutionized the production of moving vehicles—cars, boats, and airplanes.

Why digital streamlining, or spline-modeling, became such a vital concern for architectural designers—as of the early 1990s, and to some extent to this day—is less immediately evident. One frequently cited reason for this apparently baffling techno-cultural development was the overwhelming influence—particularly among young American designers in the 1990s—of the French philosopher Gilles Deleuze, whose book *The Fold: Leibniz and the Baroque* (first published in French in 1988; translated into English in 1992) suggested a relationship between computational design, parametricism, the history of differential calculus, and the curvy shapes (or "folds") that characterized Baroque painting, sculpture, and architecture. In 1996 Greg Lynn introduced the term "blob" to define the new wave of digitally modeled "Deleuzian folds," and computational splines soon came to be seen as the most conspicuous stylistic feature of the new architecture of the digital age.

MANUAL SPLINE
MODELING, CIRCA
1940
The curve (here, the
aerodynamic profile
of an airplane wing)
is obtained by
bending a wooden
slat pegged to
structural fixed
points ("ducks"),
then tracing the
curve thus obtained.

Spline evolutions: From fish to museums

A less noted, but equally relevant, part of this story had to do with fish. Frank Gehry's long-standing interest in fish, carp in particular, is well documented. Gehry's first rise to international stardom came in the aftermath of his participation in the seminal *Presence of the Past Venice Biennale* (1980)—the launching pad for international postmodernism. Yet, as Jean-Louis Cohen recently pointed out, Gehry—never a fully-fledged postmodernist—soon

Mario Carpo

In 1992 the
Golden Fish was
designed, tested,
manufactured,
transported, and
erected in the
record time of
seven months
(Permasteelisa
Group, 2015).

came to resent his accidental association with some of the historicist and revivalist topics then promoted by postmodernists; as an expression of his visceral reaction against the anthropomorphic obsession of classical architecture, he started to toy with the image of fish—after all, a much older and ancestral reference than Greek and Roman buildings, and older, in purely zoological terms, than the human body itself (Cohen, 2021; Zaera-Polo, 2006). The big metal fish he built on Barcelona's beachfront in 1992 was not his first (nor his last) but it was the first where Gehry experimented with Dassault's noted CAD-CAM software, CATIA. The connection between CATIA and fish may appear, at first, incongruous, but it follows from a perfectly rational technical argument. Fish bodies are naturally streamlined so that fish may more easily move in water. The streamlining of fish happened over time by dint, we are told, of evolutionary adaptation. But, having to build a big (184 x 115 ft.) metal fish hovering high over Barcelona's marina, Gehry observed that fish move in water in the same ways as the hull of a boat does, and concluded that the software now used to design the spliny hulls of boats should be able to emulate the natural splinliness of fish. In the end, Gehry did not find the software he needed from shipbuilders but from an aircraft maker, and the rest is history: CATIA-based spliny curves became the hallmark of Gehry's style, throughout his multifarious architectural production, and almost to this day; after the resounding success of his Guggenheim Bilbao (designed 1991–94; inaugurated 1997) the technological expertise acquired by Gehry's architectural office was spun off to an independent consulting company, Gehry Technologies (created in 2002, sold in 2014), which in 2004 released a version of CATIA specifically tailored for architectural design and became a BIM (Building Information Modeling) service provider to architectural firms around the world.

Frank Gehry, Permasteelisa, and the future of digital fabrication

If the story of Gehry's relation with Dassault is known, at least anecdotally, and it has been told many times (Carpo, 2017), nothing is known of the story of Gehry's relationship with the Italian company Permasteelisa, specializing in the project delivery of special architectural envelopes. Permasteelisa started collaborating with Gehry for the Barcelona

Fish and went on to build some of Gehry's best-known masterpieces (as well as hundreds of other very complex envelopes, curtain walls, and façades, including many designed by well-known star architects around the world). The invention of the nonstandard, postindustrial architectural envelope is then due to the unlikely encounter of a Canadian-born, Los Angeles-educated designer who managed to be at the same time anti-modern and anti-classical, with a special interest in fish; of a Paris-based aircraft maker leveraging the great mathematical tradition of French polytechnical engineering; and of an Italian curtain wall specialist that could adapt its delivery to the intention of the former, and to the technology of the latter. Gehry's panels are famously not only all curved, but also all different from one another; the "folding" draperies in the envelope of Gehry's Eight Spruce Street residential high-rise in New York City (2003–11), for example, are made of around 11,000 metal panels, but each panel has been repeated, on average, no more than five times (Permasteelisa Group, 2015, 314: the numbers cited by the company likely exclude the smaller, standard panels used for the flat cladding extending all over the southwest side of the building), and Permasteelisa's recent catalogues and technical literature pertinently highlight the Group's expertise in the delivery of irregular or complex envelopes where most components are singular one-offs. This is indeed what the digital pioneers of the early 1990s had envisaged and predicted: the nonstandard envelope of today's computer-driven global architecture is the symbol of the postindustrial logic of digital mass-customization—just as, two or three generations ago, the standardized curtain wall of high modernism symbolized the technical logic of mechanical mass-production. And just like industrial mass-production always was inherently unsustainable, digital mass-customization is, at least in theory, inherently sustainable: digital fabrication does not need scaling up to centralize manufacturing in remote, low-cost production hubs; on the contrary, the potential of digital manufacturing can be better exploited by distributed, neo-artisanal micro-factories, having access to locally sourced materials, energy, and labor. Stay tuned: the best days of the postindustrial, nonstandard architectural envelope may still be ahead of us.

GOLDEN FISH, BARCELONA
The spliny curves of this project required computer-aided design and manufacturing advancements that later became the hallmark of Frank Gehry's style.

RIGHT
IAC BUILDING, NEW YORK
The InterActiveCorp building marks the application of Gehry's language and Permasteelisa techniques to a curved glass curtain wall façade.

Mario Carpo

EIGHT SPRUCE STREET AND THE BROOKLYN BRIDGE, NEW YORK
The wavy metal façade of the Eight Spruce Street building was designed by Gehry with the support of the Permasteelisa Group.

PAGE 72
LA DÉFENSE SEEN FROM THE ARC DE TRIOMPHE

Paris

France

1970 URBAN POPULATION	2020 URBAN POPULATION	CITY PRODUCT PER CAPITA (US$)
8.21 M	11.02 M	69,768

0   1,000   2,000 m

0   5,000   10,000 ft

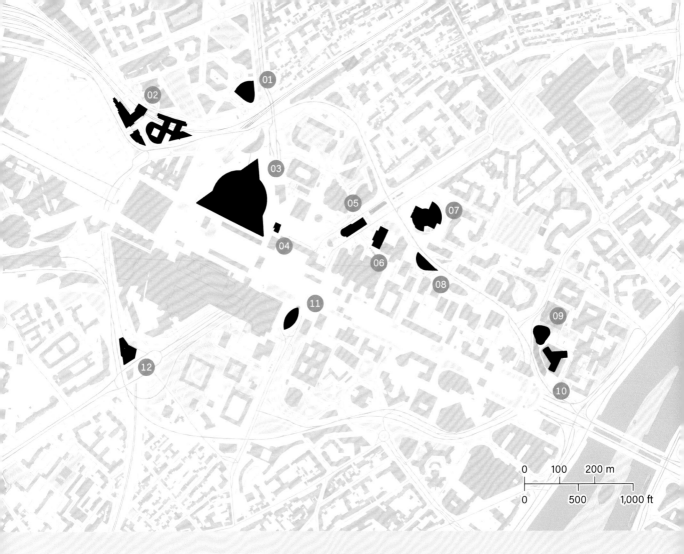

La Défense

A selection of the projects completed by the
Permasteelisa Group, name of the main architecture firm,
and year of completion.

01	Tour T1	*Valode & Pistre*	2008
02	Triangle de l'Arche	*Valode & Pistre*	2001
03	Le CNIT (renovation)	*Cuno Brullmann Jean-Luc Crochon + Associés*	2009
04	Eglise Notre-Dame de Pentecôte	*Atelier Architecture Franck Hammoutène*	2001
05	Tour Mazars Exaltis	*Arquitectonica*	2006
06	Tour Europlaza (recladding)	*B&B Architects*	1999

07	Tour Eqho (renovation)	*Hubert & Roy*	2013
08	Tour Dexia (former Tour CBX)	*Kohn Pedersen Fox Associates (KPF)*	2006
09	Tour ALTO	*IF Architects*	2020
10	Tour First (AXA)	*Kohn Pedersen Fox Associates (KPF); SRA Architectes*	2011
11	Légende (former Tour EDF)	*Pei Cobb Freed & Partners*	2001
12	Tour Hekla	*Ateliers Jean Nouvel*	2022

Paris is a competitive global city at the heart of a country where government power is centralized, and it is an important international political, economic, and cultural network. Compared with other European capitals, Paris has essentially maintained a quite homogenous urban fabric and preserved its historic landscape. Limitations to building heights and styles contributed to generating this image, which is key to tourist attractiveness—Paris is steadily among the cities with the highest number of international visitors worldwide. Since the 1960s, the national government has planned the La Défense district to experiment with contemporary building types (such as the high-rise tower) and limit their presence in the rest of the metropolitan region. Today, corporate high-rise towers like the Tour EDF by Pei Cobb Freed & Partners, Tour Hekla by Ateliers Jean Nouvel, and Tour First by KPF compose a distinct cluster in the region with other similar buildings and complexes. The repeated collaboration of Permasteelisa with large contractors like Bouygues sustained the impact of the Group over time beyond its relationship with relevant architects and design firms. This face of Paris contrasts the most stereotypical views of the Ville Lumière and perhaps lessens the recognizability of this area. Yet a wider perspective reveals the mix of historic fabric and a contemporary business district and it also helps to orient the view and recognize its geographic location; zooming into the public spaces at the base of these gigantic buildings makes one see the life behind this contemporary face of Paris.

LA DÉFENSE SEEN FROM THE GRANDE ARCHE

VIEW OF LA DÉFENSE

Frankfurt

Germany

1970 URBAN POPULATION	2020 URBAN POPULATION	CITY PRODUCT PER CAPITA (US$)
0.67 M	**0.78 M**	**69,566**

0	500	1,000 m
0	1,000	2,000 ft

Business District

A selection of the projects completed by the
Permasteelisa Group, name of the main architecture firm,
and year of completion.

01	WestendDuo	*KSP Engel*	2006
02	Die Welle	*JSK*	2003
03	OpernTurm	*Christoph Mäckler*	2009
04	Deutsche Bank	*MBA Mario Bellini Architects; gmp*	2011
05	Eurotheum	*Novotny Mähner*	1999
06	Main Tower	*Schweger Associated Architects*	1999

07	MainZero Nord (Bürogebäude Mainzer Landstraße)	B&V	2017
08	Deutsche Bank Campus Nord	KSP Engel	2017
09	DZ Bank Headquarters	Kohn Pedersen Fox Associates (KPF)	1993
10	Skyper	JSK	2004
11	Junghof (renovation)	Schneider + Schumacher	2016
12	Commerzbank Tower	Foster + Partners	1997
13	MainTor Porta	KSP Engel	2014

Frankfurt was largely reconstructed following World War II, transforming the city into a financial hub, first for Germany and then for Europe. Today, it is an important international transportation hub as well, and hosts many international companies and institutions. Crucial architectural projects like the Commerzbank Tower by Foster + Partners, the headquarters for Deutsche Bank, along with the DZ Bank Headquarters by KPF marked the image of the central business district. The Commerzbank Tower, furthermore, was the tallest building in Europe at its completion—attesting to its international stature. At the local level, the Commerzbank Tower engages with the public realm connecting with both the preexisting fabric of the surrounding blocks and several other high-rise buildings of the financial district. More recently, the European Central Bank headquarters designed by Coop Himmelb(l)au became a new icon in Frankfurt's skyline.

On these and many other occasions, the expertise of Joseph Gartner GmbH, the German subsidiary of the Permasteelisa Group, provided innovative façade technologies and solutions that characterized these companies' and financial institutions' representative towers and complexes. The latter and the city fabric of and around the central business district compose one recognizable face of contemporary Frankfurt.

VIEW OF THE BUSINESS DISTRICT

Chapter 3

The assemblage of city faces:
Transnational networks, architectural projects, and urban effects

Davide Ponzini

This chapter introduces the roles and contributions of technology providers as part of the expert networks behind the design of key buildings and areas in contemporary cities. I discuss specifically the link with architectural and urban designers while showing the recurrent collaboration with other experts involved in the creation of buildings and in transforming the city fabric.

Drawing connections between images and representations of cities like New York, London, Paris, Frankfurt, Hong Kong, Shanghai, Sydney, and others is a simple but effective way to explore how the faces of these cities have been evolving in recent decades.

This chapter intersects the broader arguments and discussions presented in this book to show that one can seek urban effects in and beyond the transnational availability of innovative technologies and technical expertise in the design and construction of selected buildings and places.

The city-face generalization trap

International exchanges and connections among cities have drastically accelerated in the last five decades. These urban dynamics are difficult to understand and visualize, despite the desire of the involved players—in global and second-tier cities especially—to promote their success in attracting new economic flows and celebrating their own city or district. Images of city development and modernization typically focus on individual iconic buildings or skylines. Skyscrapers like the Shard in London, One World Trade Center in New York, the Glòries Tower in Barcelona, as well as the buildings on the waterfront of Hong Kong or Shanghai have all played central roles in the promotional imagery of their respective cities. The same can be said about the Guggenheim Museum in Bilbao, the HQ Building in Abu Dhabi, or the Elbphilharmonie in Hamburg. The images of these buildings and places create an instantly recognizable face to the global and emerging cities of the Western and Asian world.

The spread of building types like high-rise towers or the expansion of similar urban projects such as culture-led regeneration has been explained—often too simplistically—as the inevitable outcome of globalization. Urban boosters use this argument to promote more of the same (think of the cities that followed almost literally the "Bilbao effect" narrative in the 2000s and 2010s, see Alaily-Mattar et al., 2020), while, in some academic circles, the arguments tend to blame the architectural profession, real estate developers and finance, or the capitalist system altogether (Easterling, 2005; Sklair, 2017). Within this straightforward framework, contemporary cities seem doomed to reproduce similar solutions and forms that lead—to a greater or lesser extent—to placeless images and

EIGHT SPRUCE STREET, NEW YORK
Eight Spruce Street tower's wavy façade stands out in and affects Lower Manhattan's landscape. Its aesthetics and the architect's fame are heavily publicized—one alternative name of the building being "New York by Gehry." The expertise network that made this and other innovative buildings possible often remains untold.

unrecognizable urban landscapes. In other words, the generalized argument for cities having increasingly similar faces of their central business districts and waterfront tends to downplay what actors—architects, planners, technology providers, investors, politicians, local communities, etc.—can do to improve these locales by drawing on international flows of ideas, solutions, resources, and experts.

In my view, the image that the Permasteelisa Group used in a 1999 publication of its architectural projects well represents this approach to architectural and urban globalization. This composition of more than forty buildings along one imaginary waterfront was perhaps intended to suggest the global stature of the Group and its presence in key cities across four continents. The catchphrase reads "Permasteelisa Builds the Future." At that time, the Group numbered dozens of companies with branches in twenty countries and a number of production plants responding to research and development centers with laboratories located in Europe, Asia, and Oceania. The picture displays Permasteelisa's customized solutions for quite different projects—from iconic buildings and landmarks, such as the Sydney Opera House designed by Jørn Utzon, and the Guggenheim Museum Bilbao and the Barcelona Golden Fish sculpture, both designed by Frank Gehry, to civic and cultural buildings, such as the Channel 4 headquarters in London designed by Richard Rogers or two key EU institutional buildings in Brussels and Strasbourg, as well as less recognizable office buildings and retail malls. These buildings represent varying designers in terms of profile and international reputation, from star architects like Gehry, Rogers, and Kenzo Tange, to important corporations like SOM and Architecture Studio, prominent regional figures such as Jean-Paul Viguer, and lesser-known firms. This image traces a specific transnational geography, including global cities like London, Paris, Shanghai, and Singapore as well as less specialized and connected cities like Barcelona, Bilbao, Brussels, Prague, Bangkok, and Sydney. Despite the picture having a Manhattan-like resemblance, North American cities are absent from the image as Permasteelisa was only just starting to work in that region.

This collection of buildings suffers from a level of disconnect, where some projects are self-standing in insular or peninsular development sites, and the overall lineup along the waterfront—in front of the backdrop of a dramatic sunset sky—does not compose a defined urban form. The crowded skyline fails to enhance the qualities of any specific building. It is a placeless image. The tagline added to a different version of this image "Permasteelisa Is Cladding the World" follows in the same direction: urban homogenization. Today the company seems to have gone beyond this image and underlying approach. Today's projects tend toward customized solutions and distinct aesthetics. The geographies are also changing as the competition on quality—and not on price alone—has changed over the decades and brought the Group to prefer regions with greater opportunities for higher added value and higher-quality projects.

Assemblage in place: The roles of star architects, strong-service firms, and technology providers

Of course, I am aware that one image alone cannot grasp the entire complexity of a transnational design technology provider. In addition, I recognize the long-held tradition of utilizing imaginary skylines for communication—in the eighteenth and nineteenth centuries, we find Canaletto's *Capriccio with Palladian Buildings*, Joseph Michael Gandy's *Selection of Parts of Buildings*, and Thomas Cole's *The Architect's Dream*—that may have influenced the author of the Permasteelisa image. Today, however, the transfer of projects and building features tends to be more literal than imaginary, also thanks to new design and communication technologies. An educated observer of architecture can appreciate recurring stylistic traits among the most iconic landmarks and the skylines of various cities, well beyond the evolution of the typical style of the corporate buildings or spectacular cultural facilities mentioned previously. In fact, the same set of recognizable firms often carry out these key projects worldwide. In other words, these skylines can concretely be assembled by lending certain elements and even copycats of landmark buildings (Ponzini, 2020). However, no one has so far fully investigated the

The top image is part of the 1990s communication of the Group—with the "Permasteelisa Builds the Future" tagline (Permasteelisa 1999a, 2–3). The similitude with Doha's actual skyline (in the picture below) shows the effects of collecting individual decontextualized buildings in real cities.

Davide Ponzini

contribution of design and technology service providers, not only in terms of providing shape and visual significance to individual buildings, but also in defining a larger and more complex city fabric that ultimately affects the face of contemporary cities. I argue that a generalizing or simplistic approach to these trends risks reproducing certain problems and locking cities in potentially homogenizing circuits and traps. In order to compete and stand out on a global stage, urban actors may increasingly turn to the same solutions and resort to the same designers without requiring a specific understanding of place and response to local needs and demand beyond the sole developer, owner, or anchor tenant. As an alternative, I suggest observing how specific actors operate in place, how cities transform through discrete processes and projects, and how city actors can improve specific transformations. Architectural and urban design firms are key players in this process: they provide the expertise for shaping urban transformation. At the highest levels of specialization, architectural expertise is expected to be innovative and reliable. Urban decision-makers perceive architects' provision of unique creativity and solutions for exceptional projects as a decisive factor. Firms led by charismatic designers have emerged globally, more clearly since the 1990s. However, other actors in the urban transformation process tend to value solid experience and reliability more than creativity when it comes to complex architectural and urban design and development; for example, real estate investors or developers appreciate efficiency, time, and cost reliability as these factors lead to higher profits. They tend to turn to

firms with a strong corporate image and ethos rather than to the brightest stars in the architectural firmament. Both star architects and strong-service firms typically sustain their success by expanding into multiple international markets. However, the academic debate has a limited understanding of how these most visible agents of architectural and urban design network with other local, regional, and global actors and how the latter contribute to urban transformation (McNeill, 2009). In particular, design technology providers have until now received limited attention compared to the corporate and star architectural firms that are more frequently in the spotlight. These companies providing technical know-how are an integral part of the design process today. For large-scale and complex projects, they even contribute to shaping design concepts as, more and more, efficiency and cost-related aspects are decisive in winning competitions and convincing seasoned clients. Technology providers are self-interest agents of innovation. Façade innovation often comes with more efficient and less environmental-damaging solutions (Paoletti, 2003). However, the aggregated and long-term contributions and impacts of technology providers on cities have not been investigated so far.

OPUS HONG KONG, HONG KONG
The sinuous façade of this Gehry-designed building—which was supported by Permasteelisa's expertise—gains visibility by isolation from the busy urban core of Hong Kong.

Seven cities, hundreds of buildings, and one transnational technology provider

In the introductory chapter of this book, I argued that assemblage theory helps to unpack the connections among different kinds of experts, appreciate the contributions of different actors, and see the role of material features as buildings get built in places with specific morphological, typological, infrastructural, and spatial features. This chapter explores the topic by reporting in an easily understandable manner about the presence of completed projects by the companies composing the Permasteelisa Group over time in specific cities and places. In this sense, the book's original maps, infographics, and large body of photographs provide insights and understandings of the transnational interconnectedness of urban transformation in recent decades. Global

Davide Ponzini

and second-tier cities have been intentionally chosen to articulate the proposition at the core of this book: transnational technology providers like the Permasteelisa Group play a role in changing the face of contemporary cities in cooperation with architects, engineers, urban designers, planners, and other agents that contribute to assembling complex projects in place—both distinctive projects as well as those diluted into the city fabric. Companies of the Permasteelisa Group provided different and customized façade system technologies to support medium- and high-rise residential buildings by star architects like Gehry with projects in New York (Eight Spruce Street, completed in 2011), Hong Kong (Opus Hong Kong, 2012), and more recently as part of the Battersea Power Station redevelopment in London.

Through quite distinct solutions, these projects spread common architectural and urban traits across very different situations. There have been substantial collaborations between large design firms and Permasteelisa in the selected cities; for example, KPF completed more than thirty-five projects with Permasteelisa companies in New York, London, Paris, Frankfurt, Hong Kong, and Shanghai alone. In several cases, these buildings stand out in the city fabric, like One Vanderbilt Tower in Midtown Manhattan (completed in 2020), the International Commerce Centre on the West Kowloon waterfront of Hong Kong (2010), and the iconic Shanghai World Financial Center on Pudong's Lujiazui waterfront in Shanghai (2008). In other cases, they contribute to the city fabric of central areas that are perceived as the contemporary face of these cities. Across the central business districts and waterfront redevelopment we selected for this book, one can find the same architectural firms composing the master plans and designing key landmark buildings; for example, SOM authored the plans for London's Canary Wharf redevelopment (and four of its buildings) and key buildings in

BATTERSEA POWER STATION PHASE 3A, LONDON
The Eight Spruce Street, Opus Hong Kong, and Battersea Power Station 3A (Prospect Place) buildings show various Gehry-designed interpretations of the residential tower and different solutions supported by Permasteelisa. Their façades define common traits in three disparate cities and neighborhoods.

The assemblage of city faces: Transnational networks, architectural projects, and urban effects

Lower and Midtown Manhattan such as One World Trade Center and the Columbus Circle complex, and the Jin Mao Tower for Shanghai's financial district. César Pelli master-planned Bilbao's Abandoibarra area, where the Guggenheim Museum sits, as well as the tallest building in town (Iberdrola Tower); his firm designed record-breaking buildings for height in both London and Hong Kong, along with many other cities and countries not covered in this book. In addition, these and similar transnational firms designed other relevant buildings and components of the surrounding city fabric in collaboration with the city-planning authorities. Altogether, these recurrent agents circulated their designs and solutions, informing the transformation of these contemporary places across the world. They did so together with other recurring actors.

Besides leading the master planning of the West Kowloon district in Hong Kong, Norman Foster designed the headquarters for important financial players, such as the Commerzbank Tower in Frankfurt (completed in 1997). He served its client Hong Kong and Shanghai Bank not only for the headquarters in Hong Kong (completed in 1986) but also for the headquarters in London's Canary Wharf (the HSBC Tower at 8 Canada Square, completed in 2002). These and other buildings by Foster + Partners do not only show the cooperation with the Permasteelisa Group but also the interconnectedness with the same actors that may expect these buildings to express their corporate image, cultural taste, and aesthetics in different cities. The twelve individual projects selected and discussed in this book allow for a reflection regarding the urban effects of twinned or follow-up projects. Innovative design and technological solutions contribute to shaping the façades of buildings and in some cases the visual identity of multiple cities. Visual similitudes across projects by Frank Gehry, like the Guggenheim Museum Bilbao and the Walt Disney Concert Hall in Los Angeles, or the spread of new façade technologies like those used in the Elbphilharmonie to other projects in Paris and Cupertino by different architects, are discussed in the dedicated chapters and sections. Clearly, the urban experiences in these spaces have common traits and a degree of homogenization that the pictures show.

All the seven cities selected herein tend to be depicted through their skylines. In most cases, the waterfront provides visual effects of isolation and reflection of the buildings over the water's surface, not dissimilar from the intended effect of the 1999 Permasteelisa publicity image. In cities like Paris, Frankfurt, and Shanghai, these areas evolve from development visions and derive from several-decades-long planning efforts of the local and regional planning authorities.

The planners that structured these contemporary city faces created the conditions for the collections of buildings to follow the more or less explicit archetype of Manhattan and assert analogous statements of modernity and openness to international business. Similarly to household-name architects and corporate-like firms, one may observe the same multinational firms of engineering experts supporting the creation of such buildings and complexes. Just to mention one of the most prominent structural engineering firms, Arup, one can see over sixty buildings completed in collaboration with Permasteelisa companies in the cities and projects selected for this book alone. These include key technical advancements like the Sydney Opera House, the Lloyd's Building in London and the M+ museum in Hong Kong, as well as less spectacular buildings. Likewise, the companies of the multinational WSP Group specializing in engineering count dozens of projects in cooperation with Permasteelisa of those

ONE VANDERBILT, NEW YORK
One Vanderbilt in Midtown Manhattan is one of the many landmark skyscrapers designed by KPF with façades by Permasteelisa. Among the others shown in this book, one can mention the International Commerce Centre in West Kowloon, Hong Kong, and the Shanghai World Financial Center.

Davide Ponzini

presented in this book. Over the last five decades, these and other architectural and engineering firms, together with the companies that now compose the Permasteelisa Group, worked repeatedly with multinational developers like Hines and contractors like Lendlease, just to name the most recurrent among the selected cities. These connections confirm that looking for the assemblage of expertise and their contextual effects is a promising way to identify and analyze common traits and differences across contemporary cities and central places.

These examples and those throughout the book reveal that projects tend to derive from repeat partnerships across different fields of expertise that affect the final outcome, not only in terms of architectural aesthetics but also in a wider array of urban effects; for example, the composite urban aesthetics and visual effects, the functional and mobility relations between the building and the surrounding area, and the human-scale experience in the public realm. The eventual common traits that one can detect among the cities in this book do not then depend on generic globalization trends but on specific assemblages of expertise, technologies, and solutions that circulate transnationally and occur in specific places and times. The specific characteristics may not depend only on the expert's place sensitivity but also on the urban morphology (e.g. Hong Kong's mountainous context, the tip of the Manhattan Island), preexisting infrastructure, path-dependent aesthetics, and typological features (e.g. size of urban blocks).

Resemblances among contemporary city faces

In my previous publications, I have discussed how given stakeholders and actors in contemporary cities push the spectacularization of buildings and the built environment. Typical of these trends are record-breaking skyscrapers, shiny buildings and complexes representing corporate power, iconic museums driving the regeneration of wider urban areas, and waterfront architectural compositions attracting the gaze of international tourists. Clearly, Permasteelisa and the other agents I have mentioned in this chapter have substantial roles in making these spectacles possible. At the same time, the compositional effect seems to depend, as well, on local planning powers and decisions that may achieve the intended effects of generating new icons (as for the Glòries Tower in Barcelona) or may face paradoxes like the overcrowded skyline where no single buildings manage to stand out—the City of London or the new West Bay business district in Doha are cases in point.

I have always been skeptical about and ultimately dissatisfied with grand theories aimed at explaining the transformation of cities in radically different geographic, economic, and political settings. In this sense, I do not think that innovative technologies' availability and transnational circulation alone induce urban effects such as homogenization. Nor the simple composition of projects that benefited from the expertise of the Permasteelisa companies over time in the same city can explain the evolution of that city. Similarly, I acknowledge the importance of multinational organizational, design and management technologies—like Permasteelisa Moving Forward, which, since 2008, allows different companies and teams to work simultaneously on the same project from different locations—in transferring similar solutions in geographically distant places. However, I maintain that the complex networks of actors behind these decisions and solutions are key to understanding urban transformation in context and better governing it. In my view, general trends and explanations of these processes constitute a valuable background to go more in-depth into evidence-based investigations about how architectural and urban projects, solutions, and techniques affect specific places in specific cities.

The thousands of projects completed by the Permasteelisa companies over the last fifty years constitute a pool that is sufficiently ample and articulated in space and time to allow for these and more in-depth analyses. Again, within this book, we only just begin to scratch the surface of a greater urban transformation investigation. Despite the recurrent links among transnational networks and the effects observed in the

Davide Ponzini

CANARY WHARF, LONDON
This development in London—like many others in the cities we analyzed in this book—includes multiple projects supported by Permasteelisa and designed by SOM, KPF, and other international architecture firms (see pages 48–59).

seven cities and twelve projects under observation and in the chapters herein, it is not possible to draw general conclusions about the faces of contemporary cities.

The lines one can draw across our cities and projects are similar to what Ludwig Wittgenstein calls "family resemblance" to describe common features not only among family members but also among words. The buildings and urban places are complex signifiers and some of the common traits highlighted derive from the long-term work of the companies that compose the Permasteelisa Group and their contribution to wider networks of local planners, urban designers, architects, engineers, contractors, developers, and others. Somehow, this book composes one specific transnational family picture. I believe that further systematic research can show and tell much more about these intuitions and metaphors.

**VIEW OF
HONG KONG**
During the last
decades, Hong
Kong boomed,
thanks to its
international
economic
connections. Its
high-rise fabric
and cosmopolitan
urban life rapidly
transformed the
face of the city.

PAGE 104
**VIEW OF THE
CENTRAL
DISTRICT AND
WEST KOWLOON**

102

Hong Kong

Hong Kong SAR, China

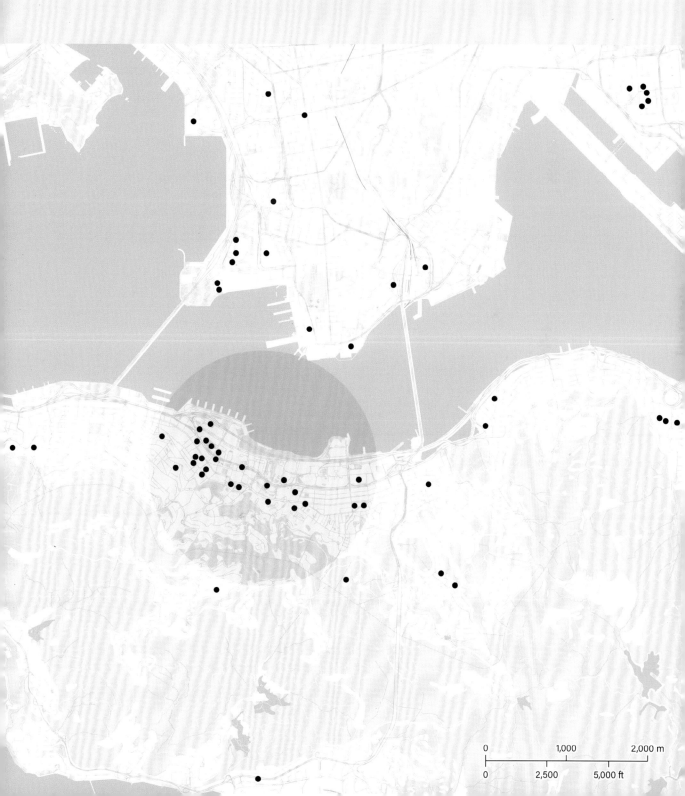

1970
URBAN POPULATION

3.40 M

2020
URBAN POPULATION

7.55 M

CITY PRODUCT
PER CAPITA (US$)

58,300

0		1,000		2,000 m
0	2,500		5,000 ft	

Central Waterfront

A selection of the projects completed by the Permasteelisa Group, name of the main architecture firm, and year of completion.

01	Two International Finance Centre	*Pelli Clarke Pelli Architects*	2003
02	The Forum (redevelopment)	*Aedas*	2014
03	Nexxus Building Link Bridge	*KLS*	2019
04	Exchange Square 1 and 2	*P&T Group*	1985
05	Jardine House	*P&T Group*	1973
06	The Putman Hotel	*MLA Architects*	2006
07	Chater House (podium)	*Kohn Pedersen Fox Associates (KPF)*	2003
08	Chong Hing Bank Centre (redevelopment)	*P&T Group*	2005
09	LHT Tower	*Rocco Design Architects*	2011
10	5-11 Stanley Street	*WMKY*	2009
11	Tai Kwun, Centre for Heritage & Arts	*Herzog & de Meuron*	2018
12	New World Centre - H2 Tower	*Ronald Lu & Partners*	2017
13	New World Centre Remodeling and Palace Mall Remodeling	*Ronald Lu & Partners*	2018

14	AIA Central	*Skidmore, Owings & Merrill (SOM)*	2005
15	Cheung Kong Centre	*Pelli Clarke Pelli Architects*	1999
16	Bank of China Tower	*Pei Cobb Freed & Partners*	1989
17	Tamar Development Project	*Rocco Design Architects*	2011
18	Pacific Place (canopy)	*Wong & Ouyang, Heatherwick Studio*	2008
19	The Hong Kong Electric Company Limited Tamar Station Building	*Kohn Pedersen Fox Associates (KPF)*	2002
20	Police Headquarters (ph. III)	*Architectural Services Department*	2004
21	Three Pacific Place	*Wong & Ouyang*	2004
22	28 Hennessy Road	*Wong & Ouyang*	2012
23	China Resources Building (renovation)	*Ronald Lu & Partners*	2013
24	Tai Yip Building	*Denton Corker Marshall*	2002
25	208 Johnston Road	*Lu Tang Lai Architects*	2021
26	One International Finance Centre (footbridges)	*Rocco Design Architects*	2000

Hong Kong served as a bridge between China and the Western world during the twentieth century. The presence of international companies and networks supported its growth to become a global economic, financial, social, and cultural hub. The high-rise and high-density fabric of many areas of the city reflects the city's success in this role. Moreover, Hong Kong has also been at the center of international tourism and one of the most visited cities in the world prior to the Covid-19 pandemic. Headquarters representing international investors and businesses have increasingly populated the skyline over recent decades. Permasteelisa's presence in the city derived from an early internationalization strategy and the development of local branches of the companies that composed the Group. The waterfront includes prominent buildings such as the Bank of China Tower by Pei Cobb Freed & Partners and Two International Finance Centre by Pelli Clarke Pelli Architects, formerly the tallest building in town during the 2000s. In addition to the original waterfront cluster of high-rises, more recently the West Kowloon district redevelopment has also included iconic buildings such as the M+ museum by Herzog & de Meuron and the International Commerce Centre tower designed by KPF, currently the tallest building in Hong Kong. The Permasteelisa Group contributed to these icons and more than seventy other projects completed since the 1980s in Hong Kong.

PAGES 108–109
HONG KONG SEEN FROM TSIM SHA TSUI

LEFT
BANK OF CHINA TOWER

TWO INTERNATIONAL FINANCE CENTRE AND THE CENTRAL DISTRICT

Shanghai
China

1970 URBAN POPULATION	2020 URBAN POPULATION	CITY PRODUCT PER CAPITA (US$)
6.05 M	27.06 M	21,785

Lujiazui, Pudong

A selection of the projects completed by the Permasteelisa Group, name of the main architecture firm, and year of completion.

01	Shanghai Foxconn Plaza (Foxconn Headquarters)	*Kris Yao	Artech*	2017
02	AZIA Center	*Kohn Pedersen Fox Associates (KPF)*	2005
03	Riviera TwinStar Square 1 and 2	*Arquitectonica*	2011
04	Pufa Tower (Shanghai Pudong Development Bank)	*WZMH Architects*	2001
05	Jin Mao Tower	*Skidmore, Owings & Merrill (SOM)*	1999
06	Shanghai World Financial Center	*Kohn Pedersen Fox Associates (KPF)*	2008

VIEW OF LUJIAZUI, PUDONG

In modern times, Shanghai has opened the door to a Western presence in China. In recent decades, the city boomed as one of East Asia's epicenters of modernization and economic growth. The skyline and landscape of the of Lujiazui, Pudong's financial district, underwent a drastic Westernization process. This is the preferred image that the government wanted to portray for the new Shanghai, to assert openness to international business and willingness to enter the club of global cities. This effect derived from the government's long-term planning effort since the 1980s to concentrate international businesses, using Shanghai—and the Pudong area in particular—as the national hub and real estate appreciation engine. The spectacular aesthetics and record-breaking heights also helped strengthen the statement while collecting specific iconic buildings such as the Oriental Pearl TV tower landmark. The Group's presence in the region was part of a long-term strategy reinforced by the city and national high-rise building boom of the 2000s. The Jin Mao Tower, designed by SOM, was the third tallest building in the world at the time of its completion in 1999. This building, along with the iconic Shanghai World Financial Center, designed by KPF, and others in this district, all used Permasteelisa's solutions.

Chapter 4

Networks of architectural production: Behind the façade of Hamburg's Elbphilharmonie

Johannes Dreher
and Joachim Thiel

Iconic architecture projects can change the perceived faces of contemporary cities. With this chapter we probe into how these projects actually materialize. In particular, we look into the geographically widespread networks of architectural production that ambitious architectural designs give rise to and that in turn render the implementation of these designs feasible.

Using the glass façade of Hamburg's Elbphilharmonie as our case study, we trace the emergence, the performance, and the consolidation of such networks that realized the concert hall and carried their experiences on to comparable follow-up ventures. Networks of architectural production, then, not only produce single projects, but also shape the faces of contemporary cities in the long run and on a global scale.

Buildings beyond the construction site

It is commonplace that buildings stick to their sites. This inherent stickiness, of course, also shapes the ways in which built structures are produced. Extant research on the construction industry therefore tends to emphasize the need for mobile factories being set up from scratch at every construction site (Bosch and Hüttenhoff, 2022). In addition, the immobility of the construction output is regarded as explaining the industry's lack of innovativeness and productivity growth (Butzin and Rehfeld, 2013). However, simply emphasizing local boundedness falls short when it comes to understanding how buildings in fact materialize, in particular with regard to iconic buildings. During the processes of designing and assembling construction projects, networks of collaboration and supply unfold that necessarily bridge different distances to the construction site. While routinized and standardized tasks tend to be available almost everywhere and can therefore usually be locally sourced, more complex, ambitious, or novel activities require widening the geographical horizon of procurement (Dreher et al., 2021). The more iconic—and therefore technically demanding and innovative—buildings are, the more they tend to engender complex and geographically stretched networks of highly specialized individuals and organizations (Boland, Lyytinen and Yoo, 2007).

ELBPHILHARMONIE FAÇADE, HAMBURG, DETAIL
The photograph displays the complexity and diversity of the façade glass panes, some of them curved, some cut open, as well as their visual pattern.

We explore and analyze how such networks of architectural production are framed and unfold; how they operate "in action"; and how they live on after a project has been finalized, carrying capabilities and technologies, but also interorganizational trust, on to follow-up ventures. Unlike most of the extant literature on iconic architectures,

The image shows the glass structure and the undulating roof surrounded by the Elbe River in the HafenCity area. The glass construction involves two flexibly borne concert halls in the center and a hotel and luxury apartments at the east and west edges, respectively.

then, we do not focus primarily on the diverse effects that these buildings have on the cities in which they are built. Rather, our main concern is on how iconic buildings in fact materialize, and how their assemblage is mutually entwined with an internationalized construction supply chain. The ambitious design of these buildings, on the one hand, generates innovation in the supply chain. On the other, only this innovation renders the assemblage of iconic buildings viable at all and thereby substantially contributes to shaping the faces of contemporary cities.

The following account is about a particularly emblematic recent case of an iconic building: the Elbphilharmonie in Hamburg, designed by the Swiss architectural office Herzog & de Meuron, and built as a crystalline glass structure on top of a 1950s brick block warehouse at the most prominent edge of the HafenCity development area. HafenCity is an ambitious waterfront development adjacent to Hamburg's city center that has substantially transformed the city's face over the past twenty-five years (Bruns-Berentelg, Walter, and Mayhöfer, 2012; Meyhöfer, 2023).

The Elbphilharmonie project was planned and built between 2001 and 2016, comprising a concert hall in conjunction with a hotel and luxury apartments and covering a gross floor area of approximately 1,351,000 square feet. From the very beginning, the spectacular design, with its crystalline appearance and the undulated roof, captivated the city's public and the local media, eventually leading to private donations of 67 million Euros. Already the image of the then future face of Hamburg unleashed a "unique dynamic" (Herzog in Mischke, 2017) that ultimately enabled the realization of the project, including the original design concept. The overall investment volume, however, amounted to 870 million Euros, after a long and conflict-laden process of cost escalations and significant delays. Our specific focus here is on the design of the façade as a spherically curved glass surface that was to both contrast the warehouse and visually interact with the surroundings, as a vivid mirror of changing water and sky conditions (Mergenthaler, Goeddertz, Grenz, and Strehlke, 2010, 45).

The research on which this chapter builds (Dreher and Thiel, 2022) is part of a larger research project on the role of large-scale projects for innovations in the construction industry (see, Thiel, Dimitrova, and Ruge, 2021). In particular, we draw on a detailed analysis of innovation processes that were triggered by the iconic design of the Elbphilharmonie (Dreher and Thiel, 2022). Besides using documentary analyses, the following pages in particular draw on the exploration of twenty-six semi-structured interviews with different professionals involved in the design, planning, and implementation of the iconic building, providing unique insights into the development process of the façade and the cooperation of key actors. We organized the material along four specific phases in the project cycle that Davies et al. (2014) regard as decisive for the introduction of innovations in large-scale projects. For the sake of this chapter, we adapt these phases, in this way considering them as also crucial for the emergence and performance of networks of production: the design phase in which the program for the network is set; the procurement phase, in which the network is composed; the implementation phase, in which the network is "in action"; and the post-project phase in which lessons are drawn and networks consolidate.

Johannes Dreher and Joachim Thiel

INTERIOR OF THE
ELBPHILHARMONIE
The picture shows
the city of Hamburg
through the glass
façade and the
printed dots fading
from the margins
to the center of the
glass panes.

Initiating networks: Design as trigger of innovations

Given the spectacular image and the positive reaction that the first renderings had triggered among the public audience, the design of the façade of the upper crystalline part of the building was of central importance. In particular, there was the general imperative of producing something "special," from the very beginning. A standard façade design would have simply been impossible, if it should meet the overall demands of the building. As one architect involved in the process explained: "One large glass building, many smooth glass surfaces. [...] That is not possible. It's a special house. It's a concert hall and a hotel and apartments. So, we have to do something with the glass. What can we do there?" As a consequence of this ambition, for the very first time the façade design involved the implementation of spherically curved four-layer security glass. What is more, the façade was to be printed and coated on different levels for the purpose of sun protection, thermal insulation, and design requirements, and the façade elements were larger in size than usually employed. Glass with these characteristics was not available on the market and had to be newly developed and customized for the Elbphilharmonie.

Assembling networks: Looking for rare experts

The design developed by Herzog & de Meuron did not allow selecting from a wide array of project partners. On the contrary, given the extreme technical complexity of the designed glass envelope, and the lack of alternative options with regard to the design, there was hardly any choice, as the contractor explained: "One knows who are the efficient façade builders [...] and there are only two, three, four who can do this in terms of quality." As the responsible project manager of Gartner, the subsidiary of the Permasteelisa Group in charge of the entire façade construction, reported in a TV documentary, "Glass bending is a specialty of two companies that can do it, worldwide. Printing, chrome is again a specialty of a company that is currently doing this for the first time" (in Schmaltz et al., 2016).

In addition, the development of the façade required technical competencies in various fields. One expert in the façade specialist company explained: "The glass was too complicated, too special" so that no company "could do it 'stand-alone.'" However, establishing cooperation between potential project partners is not a matter of course for procuring organizations, whereby the choice of partners was further restricted. Some of the potential project partners were not available as they collaborated with competing bidding consortia. Other companies did not cooperate because of previous negative experiences with potential partner firms. Some firms were hesitant because of the contractual design for the cooperation, fearing the commercial risks they would face with such nonstandard solutions, or they simply lacked the financial muscle necessary to cope with such risks. The selection that derived from all these restrictions resulted in a core group of six firms that collaboratively managed to assemble the façade. Besides architects Herzog & de Meuron in Basel, these were Gartner as the curtain wall specialist; Interpane for glass coating; BGT for printing; and Sunglass in Padua, Italy, for glass bending. Tests for break resistance were carried out in a laboratory at the University of Applied Sciences in Munich (see the map on this page).

Performing networks: Novel solutions and the imperative of design

According to one façade engineer, "the entire glass façade was a completely new procedure" in various respects. First, the production of spherically curved glass as such required a new gravitational bending technique. Heated flat glass panes had to

THE ELBPHILHARMONIE EXPERTISE MAP Map of the location of the tasks that contributed to the realization of the innovative façade of the Elbphilarmonie. The project required a transnational network and unique expertise.

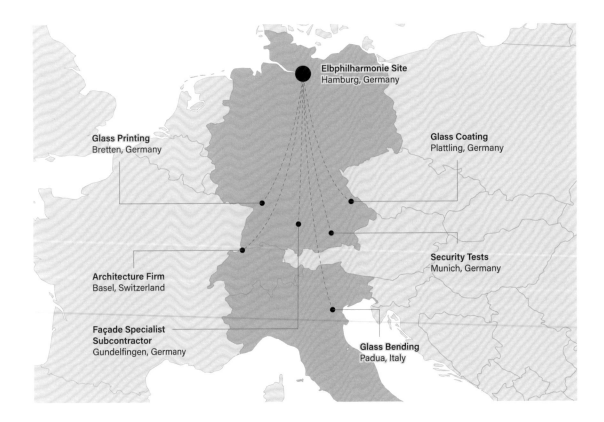

Glass Printing
Bretten, Germany

Glass Coating
Plattling, Germany

Elbphilharmonie Site
Hamburg, Germany

Security Tests
Munich, Germany

Architecture Firm
Basel, Switzerland

Façade Specialist
Subcontractor
Gundelfingen, Germany

Glass Bending
Padua, Italy

Johannes Dreher and Joachim Thiel

The 2,200
elements that
had been
manufactured in
Southern Germany
and Italy and
then traveled to
Hamburg.

sink into a tailor-made mold under their own weight. Second, the panes were larger than hitherto used so that building a new XXL oven for large-scale windows became necessary. Third, the glass panes were printed, multi-coated, and double-layered, which added complexity to the already complicated bending process. Fourth, linked to that, spherical bending also extended the heating time. Unlike with the more typical cylindrical bending where glass needs a fifteen-minute heating to 600 degrees Celsius, for gravitational bending the glass had to be heated up for about seven hours. And, "in order to protect the layers [...] the Ipachrome [the coating] that can withstand these temperatures had to be developed first" as it was explained by one expert of the glass coating firm. Fifth, there was also no empirical data on the stability of the glass panes. This lack of information made test trials necessary in order to obtain a single-use permission from building authorities for the glass elements. Sixth, novel techniques needed to be developed even for these trials. The standard test—an even load with sandbags—did not work because the bags slipped on the curved glass. Therefore, the involved test lab developed a new vacuum test with appropriate equipment. Finally, the development of the new type of façade has driven new quality criteria and assessment standards, as there were no guidelines or references with regard to defects like scratches or inclusions.

The project prompted the architects, the glass industry, and the façade builders to produce a recommendation sheet for the evaluation of spherical curved panes and the test results on the strength of curved glass panes have contributed to the development of a new standard. While the implementation process was characterized by the collective ambition of solution-seeking the objective was exclusively the realization of what the architects had designed. In the words of the glass-bending expert: "What the architects said or wanted was law," and Herzog & de Meuron made sure that their plans were implemented as intended, by monitoring the production process all way through, including quality control in the factories.

Consolidating networks: Learning and dissemination

All individuals and organizations involved in this collaboration "learned" and "grew" through the project. Each company managed to accumulate knowledge and experience about the manufacturing process; about the interplay between different glass coatings; about materials and their limitations; about parameters and statistically reliable figures on the strength of curved glass; or about the organization and risk assessment of challenging projects. In addition, and almost more importantly, the joint development of something new also enhanced the building of trust and the improvement of business relations among all team partners. The knowledge that has been created through the development process is passed on from person to person via the company network or through systematic knowledge management and can be used for following projects.

The glass coating expert explained: "[...] we still use Ipachrome now, the same stove-bent version is still in use today. We are now doing a Louis Vuitton project in Paris with it, and it has also given us a big head start. So, lessons learned, we really had a win-win situation there." The participating actors obtained a competitive advantage through the knowledge acquired and the technologies developed in the project. These added values increase their product portfolio and serve as a basis for further developments adapted to new projects, for instance the new Apple headquarters, as the Gartner project manager explained: "[...] we also use this experience for new buildings. In the last two years we built Apple's new headquarters in Cupertino. Fifty-five-foot-long donut-like curved discs that are 1,640 feet in diameter." The participating actors also benefit from their collaboration experience with project partners: Trust between individuals and also in each partner's skills grew and a common level of knowledge was formed. These aspects strengthen cooperation between companies, facilitate renewed cooperation, and enable companies to realize complex projects that would not have been accepted alone or without the necessary mutual trust.

While the knowledge about the new boundaries of what is technically feasible is disseminated in the wider industry, for instance through publications in specialized journals, concrete benefits from the innovations developed for the glass façade seem to concern mainly those actors that were actually involved in the project. In a sense, those actors were enabled to disseminate knowledge and experience as well as to leverage networks of collaboration by simply using them in concrete follow-up ventures that in turn afford their own individual imprint in the faces of contemporary cities.

Conclusion: Networks within and beyond single projects

Behind the faces of contemporary cities there is not only ambitious design by eminent architectural offices—this is what our glance behind Elbphilharmonie's façade has shown. As the key landmark building within the HafenCity development area, the design of the new concert hall does shape Hamburg's new face in a significant fashion. However, in order to translate this design into an iconic building, geographically widespread networks of collaborative production had to arise. Only through the production processes within these networks, and through the solution-seeking

TESTING
INNOVATION
The wind
stability test
on the Gartner
production site
in Gundelfingen,
Germany.

dynamics that unfold within these processes, the innovative and technically complex implementations of ambitious designs such as the Elbphilharmonie can come about.

While the networks of production are essential for the assemblage and materialization of each single building, their function for the transformation of urban landscapes does not stop with the termination of a project. Given the expertise and capabilities that the involved individuals and organizations have achieved, and given the successful experience of working together, networks live on, sometimes in more consolidated forms, sometimes in more latent forms (Davies, 2017; Dreher and Thiel, 2022). This thereby insures that the actors and networks behind the façades—including the Permasteelisa Group—will continue to shape the faces of today's cities on an international scale into the future.

NEXT PAGE
SYDNEY OPERA
HOUSE

Sydney

Australia

1970 URBAN POPULATION	2020 URBAN POPULATION	CITY PRODUCT PER CAPITA (US$)
2.89 M	**4.93 M**	**47,596**

0	750	1,500 m
0	2,500	5,000 ft

Business District

A selection of the projects completed by the Permasteelisa Group, name of the main architecture firm, and year of completion.

01	The Star	*multiple architects*	2011
02	One Darling Island	*Mirvac*	2006
03	International House Sydney (C2 Barangaroo South)	*Tzannes*	2017
04	C1 Barangaroo South	*Tzannes*	2021
05	Portico, The Scots Church Redevelopment	*Tonkin Zulaikha Greer Architects*	2005
06	2 Bridge Street	*unknown architect*	1990
07	200 George Street (EY Centre)	*fjmtstudio*	2015
08	180 George Street (Circular Quay Tower)	*Foster + Partners*	2022
09	Sydney Opera House	*Jørn Utzon; Hall, Todd & Littlemore*	1973
10	Governor Phillip Tower	*Denton Corker Marshall*	1993
11	Aurora Place	*Renzo Piano Building Workshop*	2000
12	Angel Place	*Peddle Thorp & Walker*	2000
13	8 Chifley Square	*Rogers Stirk Harbour + Partners*	2013

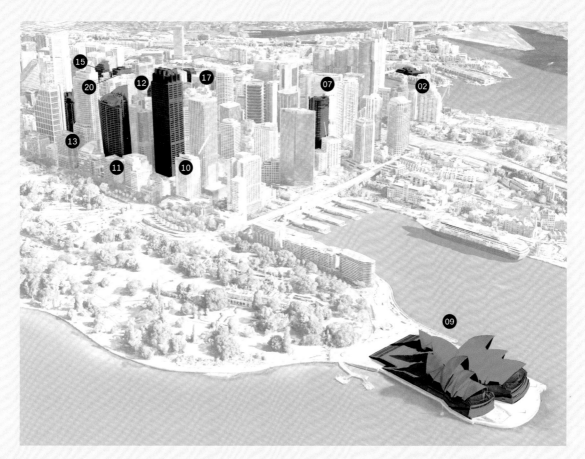

14	GPO Building (towers, 1 Martin Place)	*Buchan Group*	1999
15	400 George Street	*Crone & Associates*	1998
16	Commsec Tower (363 George Street)	*Johnson Pilton Walker*	1999
17	309 Kent Street	*Devine Erby Mazlin*	1989
18	347 Kent Street (King & Kent Street, ING Building)	*Cox Architecture*	1997
19	MMI Centre (Allianz Centre, 2 Market Street)	*Crone & Associates*	1991
20	IAG house (388 George Street; renovation)	*fjmtstudio*	2020
21	The Ribbon	*Hassell*	2021
22	Darling Walk (Darling Quarter)	*fjmtstudio*	2011
23	Fraser Suites	*Foster + Partners*	2006
24	163 Castlereagh Street (ANZ Tower)	*fjmtstudio*	2012
25	Prima Tower (338 Pritt Street)	*KANNFINCH*	1997

Sydney is a large metropolis that grew thanks to its geographical position and natural port. Today it represents an important center in the global market. The south shore of its harbor now hosts a collection of contemporary buildings, most notably the Sydney Opera House by Danish architect Jørn Utzon. This building became the city's de facto icon and a turning point in architectural history (with Permasteel providing cutting-edge technological solutions). The building's location on a peninsula also emphasizes its visual presence. However, the face of contemporary Sydney includes numerous other high-rise buildings in the nearby downtown area and business district, such as Aurora Place, designed by Renzo Piano Building Workshop, 8 Chifley Square by Rogers Stirk Harbour + Partners, the 180 George Street Tower designed by Foster + Partners, and 200 George Street by Francis-Jones Morehen Thorp (fjmtstudio), among others. The Australia-based international contractor Lendlease has been a repeat client here and in other cities worldwide. The visual composition of these and other buildings supported by Permasteelisa solutions is a prominent face of contemporary Sydney. Likewise, several projects supported by Permasteelisa solutions shaped the North Sydney high-rise cluster. After more than five decades, Permasteelisa's contribution to shaping Sydney's face is undeniable.

VIEW OF THE BUSINESS DISTRICT

Chapter 5

Transnational histories and geographies of the Permasteelisa Group, 1973–2022

Marco Antonio Minozzo Gabriel

The chapter presents an overview of the geographical development of the Permasteelisa Group from the founding of ISA in 1973 to 2022. It outlines the transnational evolutionary path of the Group, originally based in Northern Italy and then expanding its operations toward Southeast Asia in the early 1980s, to the acquisition of Permasteel, Scheldebouw B.V., and Josef Gartner GmbH and the creation of subsidiaries across four continents. During the last fifty years, the Group consolidated its presence in the Asian, European, and American markets—both following and influencing architectural and urban history.

BANK OF AMERICA TOWER, NEW YORK
The Bank of America Tower stands among the tallest landmark buildings in the city. Its design and functions derived from negotiations among developers, architects, and city planners and integrated with the adjacent Bryant Park.

A transnational "company of companies"

Important transnational paths have characterized the Permasteelisa Group's evolution. The company's main design, business, and production facilities, from its origin in Veneto to its international expansion, created a complex network that nowadays provides curtain wall and cladding technologies and products across the globe by connecting three main brands and multiple companies. The Group's geography has expanded and adapted, decade after decade, by balancing a systematic intent of internationalization and the emerging opportunities of its main product's technological and commercial characterization. Global economic and urban trends influenced these opportunities between the 1970s and 2020s, as well as the availability of expertise and partners that could advance technological provision.

Since the creation of the parent company in 1973—ISA (Infissi Serramenti in Alluminio)—the business orientation was clearly international. After the acquisition of the Australian Permasteel in 1986, the Group was renamed Permasteelisa in 1988 and consolidated its presence in the Asian market. As for its name, the whole evolution of the Group resulted from the agglomeration and joint innovation of several companies. In the words of founder Massimo Colomban at the time, the Group was understood as "a network of companies." This organizational model enhanced the flexible penetration of multiple markets while lowering corporate risk. Permasteelisa's expansion strategy has been based on acquiring other major competitors—such as the Dutch Scheldebouw B.V. in 1995 and Josef Gartner GmbH in 2000—as well as opening subsidiaries and making production agreements with third parties. The market dynamics of acquiring competitors are reflected in the company's portfolio. In the Group's internal view, purchasing other companies also meant assimilating the catalogue of their works.

Celebrating the fiftieth anniversary of Permasteelisa implies adopting the date of the foundation of ISA as a starting point; however, the acquisition of Permasteel, Scheldebouw, and Gartner, founded respectively in 1949, 1933, and 1868, extends the temporal boundaries of the Group's heritage.

Widely publicized works made by these companies before their acquisition (often before the formation of the Permasteelisa Group in the late 1980s) gained significance in defining the Group's contemporary identity. The Sydney Opera House is a case in point. Completed by Permasteel a decade before its contact with ISA, it is to this day imprinted in the Permasteelisa logo. Another significant example is the SAS Hotel in Copenhagen—which was completed in 1960 and whose façade technology was developed by Gartner. Likewise, the Lloyd's Building, completed by the latter in 1986, signified a global shift toward "high-tech architecture," ultimately characterizing the commissions in Europe that consolidated Permasteelisa's scope in the 1990s and early 2000s. In other words, rather than simply following the company's own narrative and view from the inside, this chapter analyzes the development of the Group and observes a unified "history of histories" of the different companies that merged into Permasteelisa and that jointly contributed with their expertise, heritage, and geographically articulated strategies. This approach has the purpose of making the contribution of these design technology providers more visible in time and space.

Expansions in Europe, Asia, and Oceania in the 1970s and 1980s

The technical background of these companies was formed especially in the postwar period when the standardization of modern architecture spread throughout Europe, Asia, and Oceania. The reasons why Vittorio Veneto's small aluminum sawmill industry moved toward a path of internationalization in the 1970s are diverse. To begin, the founder's vision regarding the possibilities of using aluminum for window frames, to the detriment of iron and wood, directed the company's efforts toward international commercial buildings since the Italian domestic market was resistant to its use in residential projects. The use of curtain walls in Italy was not widespread, but their technical possibilities—especially regarding flexibility, production, and installation cost reduction—became opportunities to explore the company's role beyond frame supply. Although the sale of aluminum frames was profitable, especially after "the two oil shocks that took place in the 1970s sparked a growing interest in energy conservation" (Permasteelisa, 2017, 1), the curtain wall remained at the heart of the company's business, and a tendency toward larger developments arose. The company's export share reached about 60 percent within the first decade. Personal connections and marketing through word-of-mouth drove the internationalization process more than actual advertising. This characterized an uneven geographic spread. Although Europe was the company's core market during the 1970s, work was also carried out in Iraq and Venezuela (Permasteelisa, 1988). In the early 1980s, however, the company's focus on Asia consolidated its first major act of internationalization. The cooling down of the European construction market compelled large European construction enterprises to undertake work in emerging markets. Along with them, their suppliers and longtime partners started offering their products in regions with poorly structured production chains. The development in places like Japan, Hong Kong, and Singapore, and later also in Shanghai and other major Chinese and East Asian cities, was based primarily on high-rise corporate building orders. During the period of intense development in the Asian real estate market, developers focused on high-rise towers and complexes that could be sold and rented at higher values than traditional office buildings (Garzia and Moretti, 2002). The scale of these buildings, however, challenged existing technologies. This factor, coupled with contracting large

Marco Antonio Minozzo Gabriel

North American and European architecture firms (such as SOM and Foster + Partners) for costly and innovative projects, favored the technical experimentation of skyscraper envelopes, where the curtain wall became the main distinctive element—the face of the buildings. The partnership between world-class architectural firms and the Group responded to and shaped the demand for aesthetically distinct and technically viable high-rises during economic booms.

The focus on the East and Southeast Asian market meant the need to expand the very geography of the company. The partnership with Permasteel and its subsequent acquisition established its initial foothold for the production chain. It has also become an important supplier in the Australian market itself, mainly in Sydney and Melbourne. "In 1985, the production capacity of the Italian and Australian factories totaled 100,000 square meters [about 1,076,500 square feet] per year, but toward the end of the decade, it had tripled almost reaching 300,000 square meters, thanks to the geographic partnership strategy" (Permasteelisa, 2017, 2). The company's growth is reflected in the completion of the Bank of China Tower by Pei Cobb Freed & Partners in Hong Kong in 1990, one of the most technologically daring and significant works of this decade worldwide. In the early 1990s, the Group's production structures were distributed between Veneto and Australia, although the opening of the subsidiary's office in London had already anticipated the paths followed by the Group in the 1990s.

New European business districts in the 1990s

The company's contact with renowned architects during the 1980s, as well as the experience gained in the complex commissions carried out during this decade, paved the way for the Group's consolidation in the European market in the scope of challenging projects. At the same time, the intense work in Asia continued, with some of the most notable projects with the company's involvement being completed, such as the Jin Mao Tower by SOM in Shanghai (1999) and the Two International Finance Centre (2003)

MAP OF THE
PERMASTEELISA
FACILITIES IN
1988

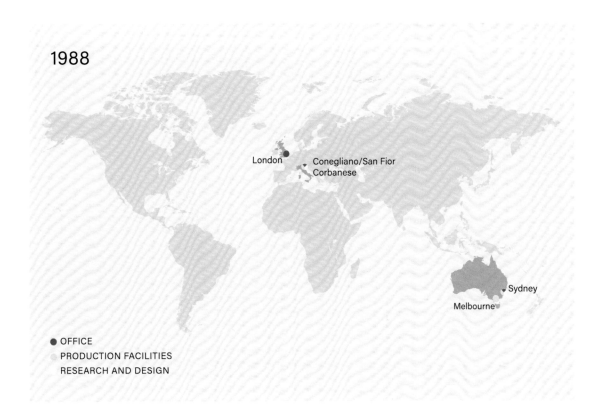

1988

London
Conegliano/San Fior
Corbanese

Sydney
Melbourne

● OFFICE
PRODUCTION FACILITIES
RESEARCH AND DESIGN

designed by Pelli Clarke Pelli Architects in Hong Kong. The 1990s witnessed a series of radical transformations in European capitals. Major projects such as La Défense in Paris, Potsdamer Platz in Berlin, and Canary Wharf in London opened space for generating new urban images in the continent's financial districts. These images were built from the insertion of high-rise architecture that, although not comparable in scale to that executed in Southeast and East Asia, pushed on technical and aesthetic experimentation, often involving star architects and firms of the late twentieth century. "By the second half of the 1990s, the level of sophistication achieved by the curtain wall, driven principally by large global manufacturers such as Permasteelisa, had profoundly transformed the competition of the metal window and door industry. The major changes had affected the contracting technology, the average size of jobs, and logistical integration" (Garzia and Moretti, 2002, 63, translated by the author).

Further geographic diversification became important to sustain the Group's growth since the Asian market had already been consolidated, and initial attempts to enter the American market by acquiring a local company were frustrated. The acquisition of Scheldebouw B.V. was essential to restructure the company's expansion strategy in Europe, which was later reinforced by the acquisition of Josef Gartner GmbH. The German company was the world's largest manufacturer of aluminum windows and doors and had always been considered the technical benchmark in the industry. The Gartner Group had a leading competitive position in the curtain wall market in Germany, the second-largest European market after the UK. The company also had subsidiaries in Eastern Europe and Hong Kong (Garzia and Moretti, 2002). This acquisition elevated the Permasteelisa Group to the world leader in this market segment. Without a doubt, Permasteelisa's most relevant work of this decade was Gehry Partners' Guggenheim Museum in Bilbao (1997). Other influential works include Foster + Partners' Commerzbank Tower in Frankfurt (1997) and multiple towers in the Canary Wharf's development. Besides the incorporation

MAP OF THE PERMASTEELISA FACILITIES IN 1999

1999

Middelburg
San Vendemiano/Fiume/ Corbanese/Treviso
London
Paris
Warsaw
Enfield/Windsor, CT
Seoul
Shanghai
Hong Kong/Foshan
Basel
Rome
Lugano
Singapore
Bangalore
Bangkok
Sydney
Melbourne
Kuala Lumpur

● OFFICE
PRODUCTION FACILITIES
RESEARCH AND DESIGN

Marco Antonio Minozzo Gabriel

of these companies' production units and research and design centers, the opening of project offices in several European capitals and important Asian centers made the company's geography more complex. At this moment, the spread of the units throughout Europe, Asia, and Oceania has operationalized a complex chain of design, production, and installation of components capable of serving a wide range of regional and international markets. From monumental works to the interiors division, the Permasteelisa Group had reached the typical configuration of a multinational company.

North America and the Middle East in the 2000s

The penetration in the American market was fundamental to the Group's growth strategy. At the end of the 1990s, the Group created Permasteelisa USA and Permasteelisa Cladding Technologies Inc. in Windsor, Connecticut. This move was consolidated with the company's purchase of Glassalum in 2003, making the Group the leader of the American national segment. The company's main area of work in the United States is New York City, where some of the most significant architectural works of the first decade of the twenty-first century are concentrated. Foster + Partner's Hearst Tower and SOM's 10 Columbus Circle, completed respectively in 2006 and 2004 in Midtown, as well as other developments in Manhattan—such as 7 World Trade Center by SOM and Gehry's IAC Building (both completed in 2006 and 2007 respectively)—consolidated Permasteelisa's reputation in North America. In Europe, Jean Nouvel's Glòries Tower in Barcelona (2005) reflected European cities' verticalization push and search for new architectural landmarks. Besides completing many important works during the 2000s in Asia, Europe, and the USA, the Group decided to reinforce its Middle East presence, particularly in Dubai, "where the economic boom and the increase in construction was linked to the local government's decision to focus [the city's …] economy on tourism and services instead of petroleum" (Permasteelisa, 2017, 6). The completion of the HQ Building—the headquarters of Aldar, one of the Emirate's leading

MAP OF THE
PERMASTEELISA
FACILITIES IN
2010

2010

OFFICE
PRODUCTION FACILITIES
RESEARCH AND DESIGN

real estate developers—in 2010 in Abu Dhabi represents this tendency. The great complexity of the Permasteelisa Group's design and production department required an efficient and effective management system. In 2008, the Group invested heavily in creating an integrated management system to handle all the work phases, from architectural development to installation, including design, engineering, production, and maintenance. This led to the creation of Permasteelisa Moving Forward (PMF), a process management tool that allows multiple Group companies and teams to work simultaneously on the same project from different offices and locations. Today, PMF constitutes the Group's proprietary BIM (Building Information Modeling) platform. It enables the dialogue and information share with all the BIM platforms available on the market today. This process reduces the information loss and allows for greater integration between the Group companies and teams and across the various project and work phases (Permasteelisa, 2017).

Global presence in the 2010s

In 2011, after opening its capital to private equity funds, Permasteelisa was acquired by the Japanese multinational Lixil Corporation. Subsequently, it became the core of Lixil's Building Technology business unit, coordinated from the Vittorio Veneto office (Vedovato et al., 2021). In the following years, it expanded the Group's manufacturing yard and office network to its maximum size. In 2016, the billion-dollar turnover company had over 6,000 employees, distributed in about fifty companies and thirty countries worldwide, with an annual production of about about 1,076,500,000 square feet of curtain wall surface. The Group's reorganization into four macro-regions in 2016—America, Europe, the Middle East, and Asia—reflects this administrative complexity.

The works carried out worldwide, reflected the company's ever-growing focus on highly innovative and challenging projects. In addition, the new boom in the high-rise segment in cities like London (with works like Renzo Piano's Shard, 2012), Milan (with Pelli's UniCredit Tower, 2012) and Frankfurt, and the constant demand for skyscrapers in Asian megalopolises and New York, and other complex projects such as architects Herzog & de Meuron's Elbphilharmonie in Hamburg (2016), widened Permasteelisa's technical scope and expertise. Likewise, the long-standing partnerships between the Group and world-class architectural firms kept moving technological advancements from one continent to another just as it affected these cities' faces, as one can perceive in examples such as the M+ museum, completed by the same Herzog & de Meuron firm in Hong Kong's West Kowloon district in 2021.

PERMASTEELISA MOVING FORWARD
The Permasteelisa Moving Forward (PMF) software provides a unified global information system for the projects developed by the Group. This Building Information Modeling technology allows for a streamlined flow of digital information—from the early stages of inquiry and design of façades to their manufacturing, installation, and maintenance.

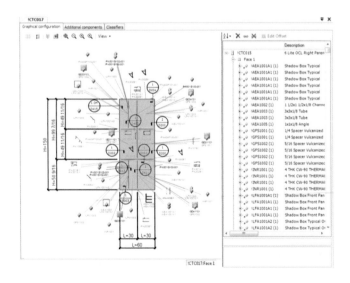

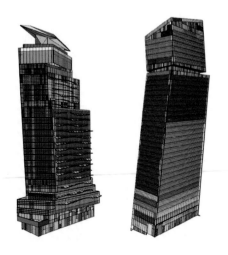

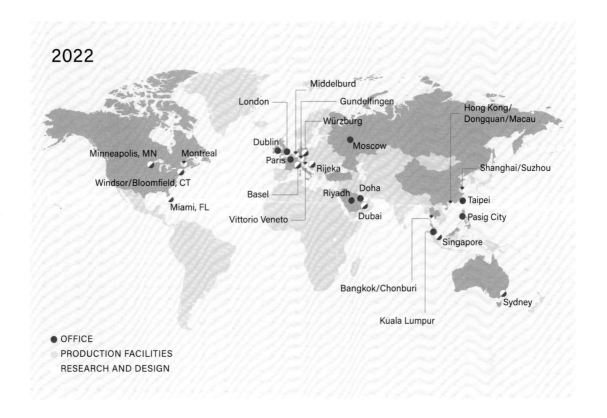

2022

Minneapolis, MN
Montreal
Windsor/Bloomfield, CT
Miami, FL
London
Middelburd
Gundelfingen
Würzburg
Dublin
Paris
Moscow
Rijeka
Basel
Riyadh
Doha
Vittorio Veneto
Dubai
Hong Kong/ Dongquan/Macau
Shanghai/Suzhou
Taipei
Pasig City
Singapore
Bangkok/Chonburi
Kuala Lumpur
Sydney

● OFFICE
PRODUCTION FACILITIES
RESEARCH AND DESIGN

MAP OF THE
PERMASTEELISA
FACILITIES IN
2022

Networking and strategic directions

In recent years, a substantial readjustment of the structure and logistics chain of the Group—which has been part of Atlas Holdings since 2020—occurred. The Group strategically reduced the number of offices to focus on highly complex projects in specific countries and markets where the Group can have a competitive advantage based on its advanced technological skills and knowledge. The interiors division now operates in Asia only. The curtain wall sector remains the core business, focusing primarily on markets with high added value. Through its geographical, economic, and digital configurations, the Permasteelisa Group's transnational trajectories necessarily responded to the geopolitical transformations of the intense period of globalization between the end of the twentieth century and the beginning of the twenty-first century. The Group had to strategically navigate through booms and bursts in different world regions and increasingly prioritized innovation, quality work, and technical expressiveness. This reflects an almost symbiotic relationship between the Group and large architecture and engineering firms and repeat cooperation with large contractors in different countries and regions. In this relationship, the design of façades with its fundamental role in constructing the architectural discourse is an interactive and cooperative process in which the roles of supplier and designer overlap beyond the technical feasibility of constructive solutions. Reliability and expertise in navigating uncharted architectural and engineering waters motivate contractors to keep working with Permasteelisa for their most innovative projects.

Observing the transnational geographies and histories of the Permasteelisa Group over the last fifty years helps one not only see the evolution of high-rise buildings and architecture more generally, but also understand given common traits among the faces of contemporary cities.

Selected projects

SAS Royal Hotel

Copenhagen 1960

The SAS Royal Hotel was commissioned to architect Arne Jacobsen by the SAS Scandinavian Airlines in 1955 as a hotel and a terminal with integrated check-in counters. It was Denmark´s tallest skyscraper at the time of completion (1960), raising criticism regarding the implementation of high-rise architecture in traditionally low-rise urban contexts. It is one of the most important projects by the Permasteelisa Group company Josef Gartner GmbH. The international style echoed the SOM-designed Lever House (1952), the second-ever skyscraper with a glass curtain wall built in New York City.

The standardization of architecture and the industrialized mass production of building elements were essential in advancing and transferring façade technologies and expanding the business of Gartner that subsequently became one of the world's largest providers of aluminum and glass façades in the following decades. This project is a possible European response to the American high-rise glass-façade type. Here Jacobsen's personal design language is visible in the building's interiors (see the Room 606 original design in the picture below), volumes, and overall form.

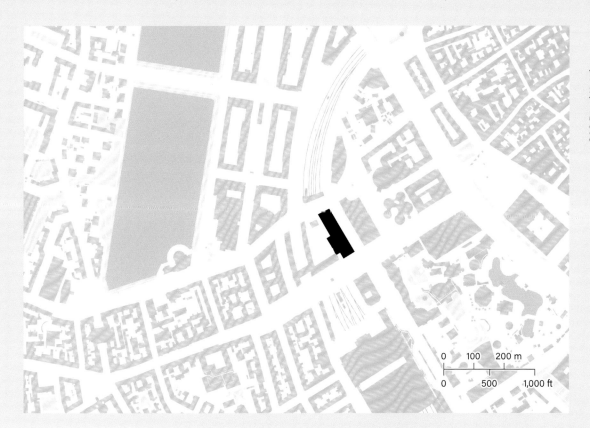

LOCATION	Copenhagen, Denmark
YEAR OF COMPLETION	1960
HEIGHT	228 ft.
COST OF CONSTRUCTION	US $4.3M
ARCHITECT	Arne Jacobsen
STRUCTURAL ENGINEER	Kampsax A/S
FAÇADE TECHNOLOGY PROVIDER	Gartner
MAIN CONTRACTOR	Kampsax A/S
DEVELOPER	Scandinavian Airlines Systems (SAS)
OWNER	Radisson Hotel Group
MAIN TENANT	Radisson Collection Royal Hotel

Sydney Opera House

Sydney 1973

Since its opening in 1973, the Sydney Opera House has established itself as the main landmark of Sydney Harbour. The building is visually unmissable thanks to its isolation on a peninsula and bold volumes. It has become one of the city's main tourist destinations. Its construction required revolutionary engineering and building techniques and the advanced expertise of architect Jørn Utzon, engineer Ove Arup, and the Permasteel team. The pioneering use of structural silicone and suspended vertical glass on a large scale— the central bay is about 112 feet long and suspended without any intermediate supports—was realized by Permasteel, a company that later merged into the Group. These and other advancements are also reflected in the backdrop of medium- and high-rise buildings found beyond the Sydney Opera House. Several high-rise towers whose façades were executed by Permasteelisa in the last fifty years benefited from technologies consolidated in this groundbreaking work, both in Sydney and across other international contexts. In 2007 the Opera House gained UNESCO World Heritage Site status as a "masterpiece of late modern architecture that pushed architecture and engineering to new limits."

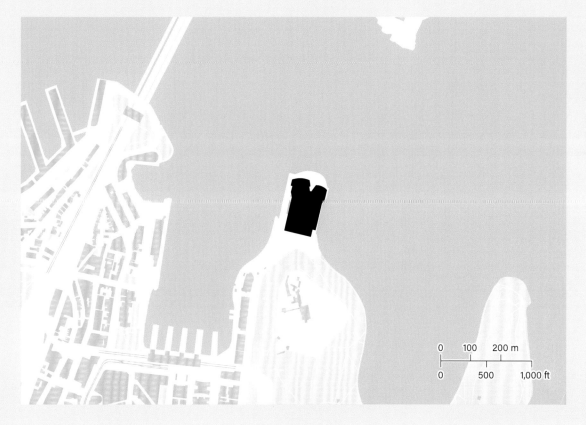

LOCATION	Sydney, Australia
YEAR OF COMPLETION	1973
SURFACE	194,000 sq. ft.
HEIGHT	220 ft.
COST OF CONSTRUCTION	US $130M
ARCHITECTS	Jørn Utzon; Hall, Todd & Littlemore
ARCHITECT OF RECORD	Hall, Todd & Littlemore
STRUCTURAL ENGINEER	Ove Arup & Partners
FAÇADE TECHNOLOGY PROVIDER	Permasteel
MAIN CONTRACTORS	Lendlease; Manuel Hornibrook
DEVELOPER	New South Wales Department of Public Works
OWNER	New South Wales Government
MAIN TENANTS	Opera Australia; The Australian Ballet; Sydney Theatre Company; Sydney Symphony

Lloyd's Building

London 1986

When it was built, the Lloyd's Building bore the key features of so-called "high-tech architecture." Beyond its controversial aesthetics, this project and its innovative solutions reinforced Rogers's figure as a world-class architect and his use of high-tech language. The structure and façade system were visible parts of the innovation. They benefited from the contribution of, respectively, Ove Arup engineering company and Josef Gartner GmbH (which later merged into the Permasteelisa Group). Shortly thereafter, in 1994, Rogers designed the Channel 4 Television Building, also located in London: the latter follows similar aesthetic choices highlighting the structural elements, a solution earlier adopted in the Lloyd's Building. Projects by other architects like Renzo Piano and Norman Foster also incorporated similar features. Central business districts in cities such as Frankfurt, Berlin, New York, Hong Kong, and Shanghai all include buildings influenced by Rogers's work.

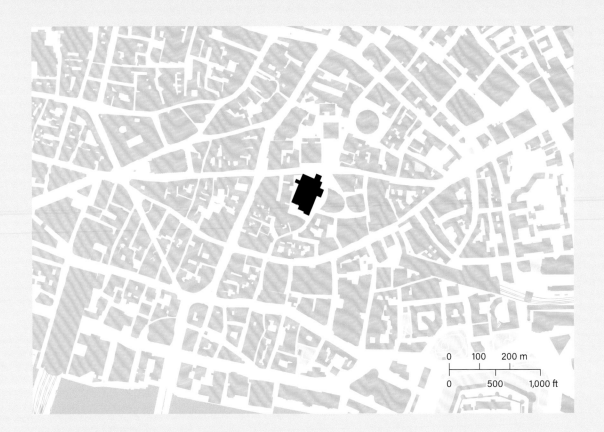

LOCATION	London, UK
YEAR OF COMPLETION	1986
SURFACE	592,000 sq. ft.
HEIGHT	276 ft.
COST OF CONSTRUCTION	US $108M
ARCHITECT	Rogers Stirk Harbour + Partners
STRUCTURAL ENGINEER	Ove Arup & Partners
FAÇADE TECHNOLOGY PROVIDER	Gartner
MAIN CONTRACTOR	Bovis Construction Ltd
OWNER	Ping An Real Estate Co Ltd
MAIN TENANT	The Lloyd's Corporation

Bank of China Tower

Hong Kong 1990

The 1,206-foot-high Bank of China Tower, completed in 1990, is quite symbolic of the rise of Asian economies in the 1980s and was one of the tallest towers in the world at its inauguration. It is a typical example of the high-rise headquarters of a financial institution that became a vast field of exploration for curtain wall façades in the major global financial centers of the last decades of the twentieth century. Gartner and Permasteelisa played a key role in this development and expansion, supplying and testing new technologies that allowed for the innovation of this tower and vertical growth in Asian megalopolises such as Hong Kong, Shanghai, and Singapore. The Asian collaborations between companies of the Permasteelisa Group and multinational design firms (typically headquartered in Europe and North America) between the 1980s and 1990s were later reproduced in partnerships for financial district projects in Europe, such as at Canary Wharf in London, La Défense in Paris, and Potsdamer Platz in Berlin. These combinations of technical solutions and aesthetics would then spread to cities in other regions like the Middle East.

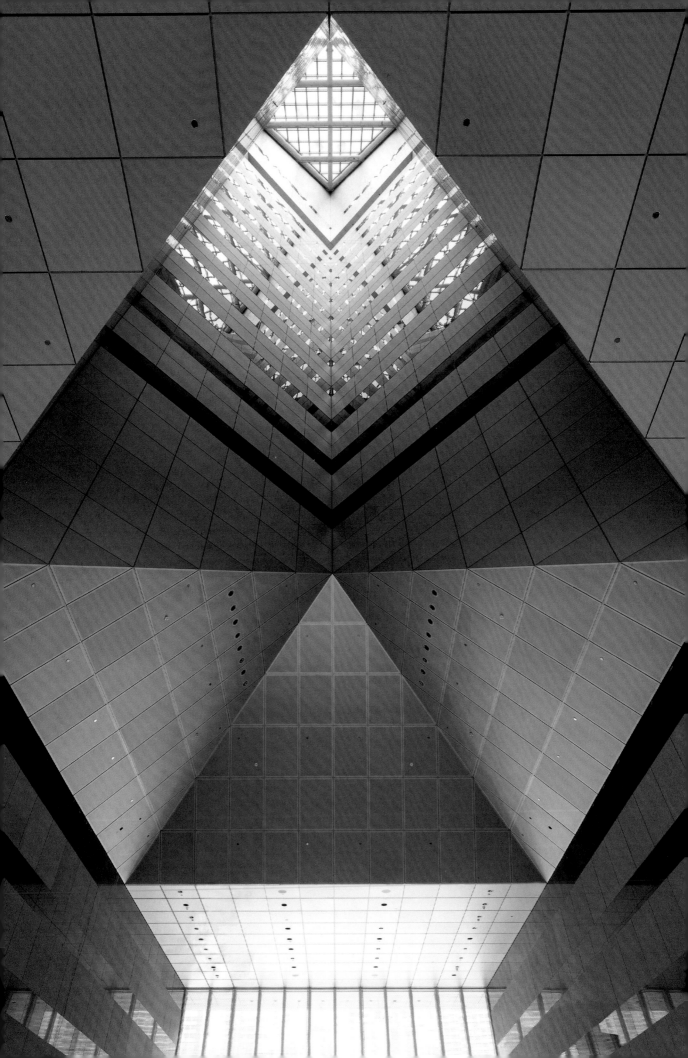

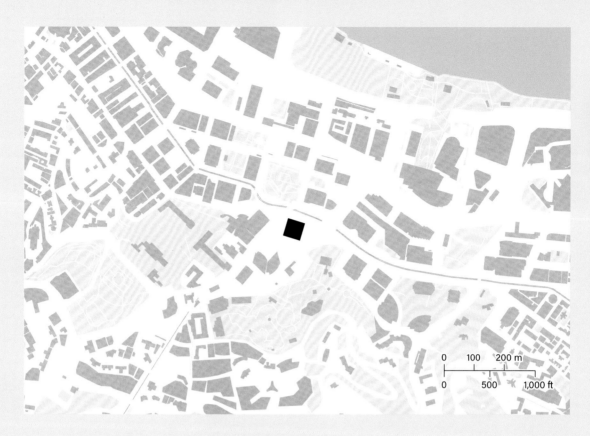

LOCATION	Hong Kong SAR, China
YEAR OF COMPLETION	1990
SURFACE	1,400,000 sq. ft.
HEIGHT	1,206 ft.
COST OF CONSTRUCTION	US $130m
ARCHITECT	Pei Cobb Freed & Partners with Sherman Kung & Associates Architects
STRUCTURAL ENGINEER	Leslie E. Robertson Associates RLLP
FAÇADE TECHNOLOGY PROVIDER	Gartner
MAIN CONTRACTOR	Kumagai Gumi Co Ltd
DEVELOPER	Bank of China
OWNER	Bank of China
MAIN TENANT	Bank of China

Guggenheim Museum
Bilbao

Bilbao 1997

The Guggenheim Museum Bilbao opened in 1997 and became the iconic representation of a broader process of urban regeneration of the city and region. Its bold architectural forms and façade solutions resulted from the collaboration between Gehry Partners and Permasteelisa. Drawing on the experience of an existing partnership for the design of the Golden Fish for the 1992 Barcelona Olympic Games, the Group and the architects used CATIA software to realize the complex flow of the building's titanium skin. Permasteelisa helped design and produce the different panel shapes, ensuring alignment throughout the complex wall curvatures. The success of this partnership has been replicated in other prominent projects, notably in the Walt Disney Concert Hall in Los Angeles (see page 62), whose design ran almost parallel to the Guggenheim Museum Bilbao and which shares similar design features. The design and aesthetics of many other museums worldwide have been inspired by these forms and solutions since.

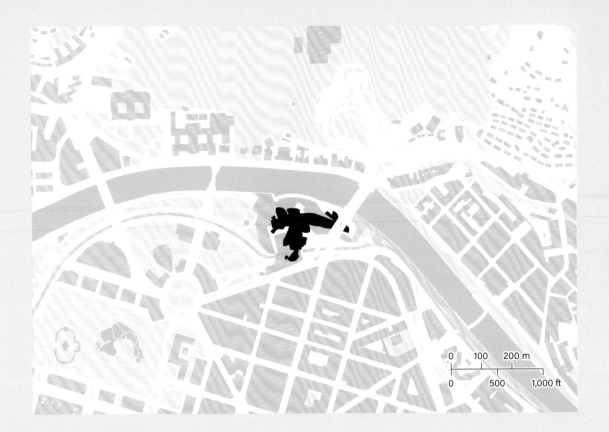

LOCATION	Bilbao, Spain
YEAR OF COMPLETION	1997
SURFACE	258,000 sq. ft.
COST OF CONSTRUCTION	US $89M
ARCHITECT	Gehry Partners
ARCHITECTS OF RECORD	César Caicoya Gómez-Morán; José Antonio Amann Murga; Aitor Azcárate Gómez
STRUCTURAL ENGINEER	Skidmore, Owings & Merrill (SOM)
FAÇADE TECHNOLOGY PROVIDER	Permasteelisa
MAIN CONTRACTOR	Bolzola
OWNER	Solomon R. Guggenheim Foundation
MAIN TENANT	Solomon R. Guggenheim Foundation

Glòries Tower

Barcelona 2005

The Glòries Tower, formerly known as Agbar Tower (from the city's water utility company), sits in a very visible point of the city fabric: Plaça de les Glòries Catalanes, at the crossroads of three main road axes. Jean Nouvel's design covered the reinforced concrete shell with a skin composed of thousands of glass components. By night, the building envelope's visual effect is reinforced by LED lighting devices. The complex façade system benefited from Permasteelisa's expertise. The iconic building has become a new landmark for Barcelona and represents the regeneration of the Poblenou area. During the 2000s, this former industrial neighborhood underwent extensive transformations and now hosts a set of new cultural, office, and residential spaces. Poblenou's medium-rise and grid-aligned urban fabric was planned to enhance the prominence of the Glòries Tower.

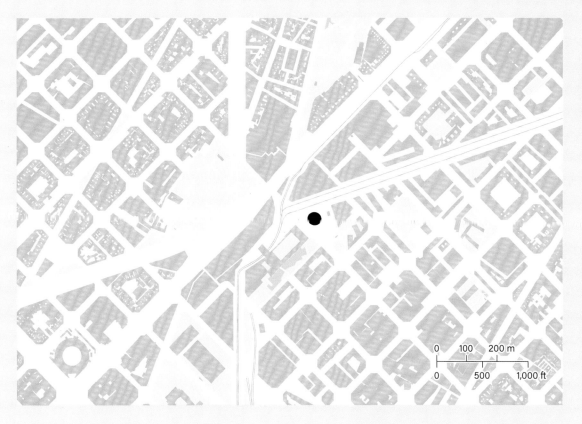

LOCATION	Barcelona, Spain
YEAR OF COMPLETION	2005
SURFACE	511,300 sq. ft.
HEIGHT	474 ft.
COST OF CONSTRUCTION	US $177M
ARCHITECT	Ateliers Jean Nouvel
ARCHITECT OF RECORD	B720 Fermín Vásquez Arquitectos
STRUCTURAL ENGINEERS	Robert Brufau y Associados; Obiol Moya y Associados
FAÇADE TECHNOLOGY PROVIDER	Permasteelisa
MAIN CONTRACTOR	Layetana
DEVELOPER	Layetana
OWNER	Merlin Properties
MAIN TENANT	Agbar Group

Hearst Tower

New York 2006

Hearst is a multinational media corporation headquartered on Eighth Avenue in Midtown Manhattan. Creating the new tower involved the redevelopment of a building from 1928, providing a unique image and a more efficient and sustainable seat of operations. The corporation selected architect Norman Foster for his expertise in dealing with historic buildings, technological competence, and sustainability orientation. The futuristic aesthetics of the Hearst Tower, completed in 2006, owe much to the innovative external cladding supplied by the Permasteelisa Group. The main feature is a diagonal grid of stainless-steel elements and glass panels covering the building's structure that creates a discernable triangular pattern. The building is highly visible from different locations in the city, including Central Park.

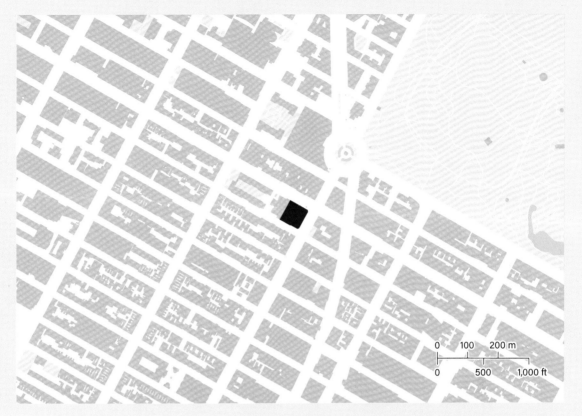

LOCATION	New York City, USA
YEAR OF COMPLETION	2006
SURFACE	856,000 sq. ft.
HEIGHT	597 ft.
COST OF CONSTRUCTION	US $500M
ARCHITECT	Foster + Partners
ARCHITECTS OF RECORD	Adamson Associates Architects
STRUCTURAL ENGINEER	WSP Cantor Seinuk
FAÇADE TECHNOLOGY PROVIDER	Permasteelisa
MAIN CONTRACTOR	Turner Construction
DEVELOPER	Tishman Speyer
OWNER	Hearst Corporation
MAIN TENANT	Hearst Communications

HQ Building

Abu Dhabi 2010

In many ways, the HQ Building symbolizes the radical transformation of contemporary Abu Dhabi, the capital of the United Arab Emirates. The building is the headquarters of Aldar, the leading real estate developer in the region. In 2010, it was the first completed project of the massive Al Raha development along the coast just off the main island of Abu Dhabi, located on the way to the international airport. As an isolated large-scale element, the HQ Building confirmed that the large-scale and fast-track transformation of the region envisioned in the 2000s was possible. Permasteelisa supported this and several other key projects in booming cities of the region like Doha, Dubai, and more recently Riyadh. The Lebanese designer of the HQ Building, MZ & Partners, worked extensively in the region and completed other iconic projects in Doha that used similar aesthetics.

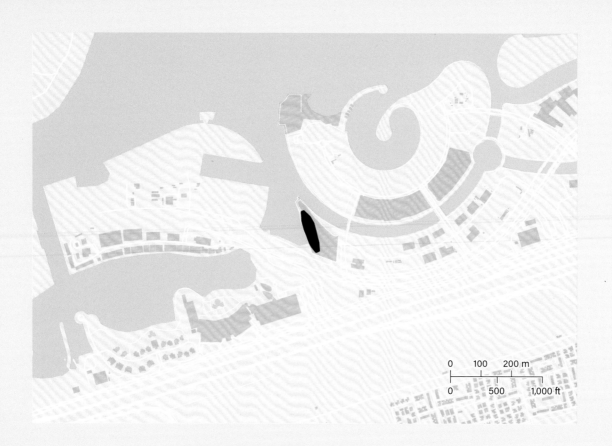

LOCATION	Abu Dhabi, UAE
YEAR OF COMPLETION	2010
HEIGHT	397 ft.
ARCHITECT	MZ & Partners
STRUCTURAL ENGINEER	Arup
FAÇADE TECHNOLOGY PROVIDER	Permasteelisa
MAIN CONTRACTORS	Aldar; Laing O'Rourke Construction
DEVELOPER	Aldar
OWNER	Aldar
MAIN TENANT	Aldar

193

The Shard

London 2012

The Shard responds to a season of densification of infrastructural hubs and central areas in London that started in the 2000s. This ninety-five-story tower is located near the London Bridge station. The Renzo Piano Building Workshop went through multiple versions to better accommodate the complexities of mobility and public space at the foot of the building and to achieve a dramatic visual effect in a central area of London. The technical feasibility of this kind of high-rise project required the evolution of curtain wall technology and the streamlining of its production, installation, and maintenance. The eight glass "shards" that compose the building's overall shape remain independent and never touch one another, a technical solution to reduce overall wind load. A mixed-use tower, often referred to as the "vertical city," the Shard is the tallest building in the United Kingdom and has become not only the new face for a string of transformations on the Thames South Bank, but also a new landmark for the whole city of London.

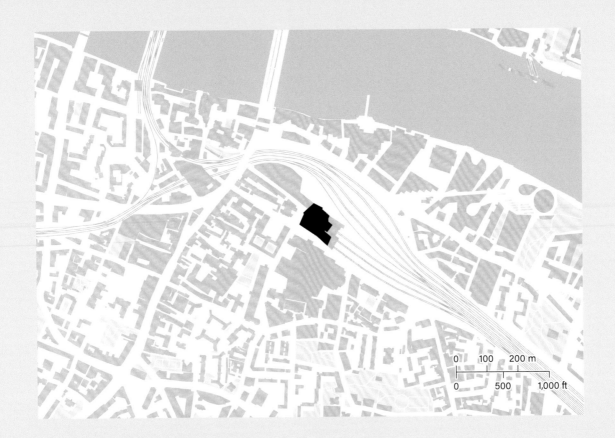

LOCATION	London, UK
YEAR OF COMPLETION	2012
SURFACE	1,363,800 sq. ft.
HEIGHT	1,015 ft.
COST OF CONSTRUCTION	US $675M
ARCHITECT	Renzo Piano Building Workshop
ARCHITECT OF RECORD	Adamson Associates Architects
STRUCTURAL ENGINEER	WSP Cantor Seinuk
FAÇADE TECHNOLOGY PROVIDER	Scheldebouw
MAIN CONTRACTOR	Mace
DEVELOPER	Sellar Property
OWNERS	Qatar Investment Authority; Sellar Property
MAIN TENANTS	multiple

UniCredit Tower

Milan 2012

The UniCredit Tower complex is the Milan headquarters of the UniCredit multinational bank. It comprises three towers. The spire of the tallest building reaches 758 feet, making it the tallest building in Italy. After completion in 2012, the complex became a landmark for the Porta Nuova business district and the whole city. The curvilinear façades generate a circular public space (Piazza Gae Aulenti) with a diameter of approximately 328 feet. The piazza's proportions and the inclined canopy that runs along the buildings tame the perception of the height and size of the complex and support the liveliness of the commercial frontage. A 19-foot-tall podium raises the whole area above the original street level and contains a large retail and parking space, connected to the adjacent Porta Garibaldi station. This typological choice is not common in the Milanese context. The image of the project leans toward an international and spectacular aesthetic and tends to homogenize the complex within the global urban panorama.

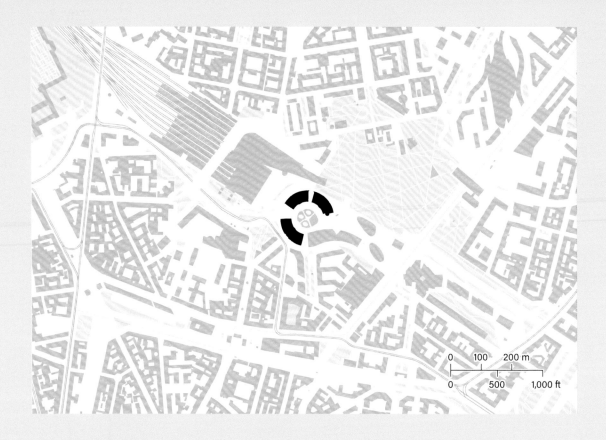

LOCATION	Milan, Italy
YEAR OF COMPLETION	2012
SURFACE	1,410,000 sq. ft.
HEIGHT	758 ft.
COST OF CONSTRUCTION	US $248M (including podium)
ARCHITECT	Pelli Clarke Pelli Architects
ARCHITECTS OF RECORD	Adamson Associates International
STRUCTURAL ENGINEER	Alpina and MSC Associati
FAÇADE TECHNOLOGY PROVIDER	Permasteelisa
MAIN CONTRACTOR	Colombo Costruzioni
DEVELOPER	Hines Italia
OWNER	Qatar Investment Authority
MAIN TENANT	UniCredit

Elbphilharmonie

Hamburg 2016

The Elbphilharmonie building, completed in 2016, contributed to the regeneration of a rapidly changing quadrant of Hamburg, the former dockyards of HafenCity. The project was sponsored by segments of Hamburg society but also raised public concerns regarding its feasibility and cost. The reuse of the "Kaispeicher" heritage building, originally a warehouse, required advanced design expertise. The envelope of this building became a test bed for new glass-bending techniques, particularly in the double-curved glass panels that characterize the façade and distinct exteriors. The Permasteelisa Group embraced this challenge by developing new solutions that have subsequently become available for other projects. Architects have since collaborated with Permasteelisa companies using these technologies for new projects, such as in the Foster-designed Apple headquarters in Cupertino.

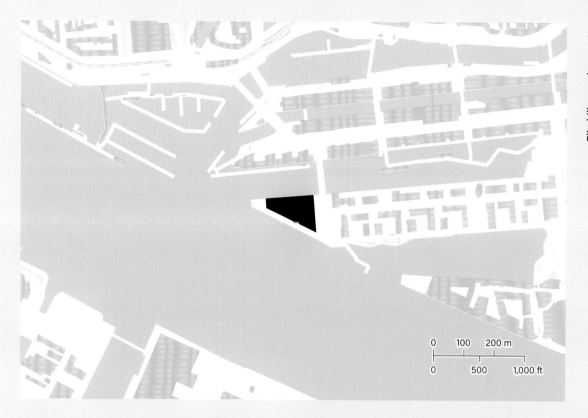

0   100   200 m

0   500   1,000 ft

LOCATION	Hamburg, Germany
YEAR OF COMPLETION	2016
SURFACE	1,351,000 sq. ft.
HEIGHT	361 ft.
COST OF CONSTRUCTION	US $943M
ARCHITECT	Herzog & de Meuron
ARCHITECTS OF RECORD	H+P Planungsgesellschaft mbH & Co; KG
STRUCTURAL ENGINEER	Schnetzer Puskas International AG; Heinrich Schnetzer
FAÇADE TECHNOLOGY PROVIDER	Gartner
MAIN CONTRACTOR	Hochtief Solutions AG
DEVELOPER	Freie und Hansestadt Hamburg
OWNERS	Freie und Hansestadt Hamburg, Germany, represented by Elbphilharmonie Hamburg Bau GmbH & Co
MAIN TENANT	Elbphilharmonie Hamburg

Hong Kong 2021

The M+ museum designed by Swiss architects Herzog & de Meuron is the crown jewel of a vast master plan in the harbor basin of Hong Kong. The plan involved the controversial redevelopment of a historic neighborhood and included large infrastructure investments for the West Kowloon Cultural District. The master plan and the M+ project were aimed at strengthening Hong Kong as a cultural center and tourist destination, boosting its visibility and media exposure. The M+ museum was completed in 2021 and now hosts an international collection of twentieth- and twenty-first-century visual culture, with a focus on Hong Kong but also with important artifacts of international origin. The building stands in front of Victoria Harbour and uses its main façade as a large screen—the panels lining the building's façade facing the harbor contain grooves for inset LED lights. This and other innovative technological solutions were supported by the collaboration with Permasteelisa and allowed for a spectacular effect visible from many vantage points in Hong Kong.

LOCATION	Hong Kong SAR, China
YEAR OF COMPLETION	2021
SURFACE	995,000 sq. ft.
HEIGHT	308 ft.
COST OF CONSTRUCTION	US $770M
ARCHITECT	Herzog & de Meuron
ARCHITECTS OF RECORD	TFP Farrells
STRUCTURAL ENGINEER	Arup
FAÇADE TECHNOLOGY PROVIDER	Permasteelisa
MAIN CONTRACTOR	Blue Poles Limited (BPL)
DEVELOPER	West Kowloon Cultural District Authority
OWNER	West Kowloon Cultural District Authority
MAIN TENANT	M+

Appendix

About the authors

Mario Carpo

Mario Carpo is an architectural historian and critic, currently the Reyner Banham Professor of Architectural History and Theory at the Bartlett, University College London and the Professor of Architectural Theory at the Institute of Architecture of the University of Applied Arts (die Angewandte) in Vienna. His research and publications focus on history of early modern architecture and on the theory and criticism of contemporary design and technology. He is the author of *Beyond Digital: Design and Automation at the End of Modernity* (MIT Press), *Architecture in the Age of Printing* (MIT Press), among other books.

Johannes Dreher

Johannes Dreher has a PhD from the Technical University of Munich (TUM, School of Engineering and Design). He works in the Department of Integrated Urban Development of the City of Hamburg. He was previously a research associate at the HafenCity University Hamburg (HCU) and the Technical University of Munich (TUM), where he was part of interdisciplinary research projects investigating innovations in large-scale construction projects (HCU) and the effects of star architecture projects on urban development (TUM). Dreher has also worked as a Research Analyst at CBRE GmbH in Frankfurt.

Marco Antonio Minozzo Gabriel

Marco Antonio Minozzo Gabriel received his PhD degree in Conservation of the Architectural Heritage from Politecnico di Milano in 2023. Previously, he worked for the Brazilian Ministry of Culture as a chief of a technical Office of IPHAN—National Institute of the Historical and Artistic Heritage. He has worked in multiple capacities as architectural historian, focusing primarily on transnational contexts and technological transferences between Europe and Brazil.

Davide Ponzini

Davide Ponzini is a Full Professor of Urban Planning and the director of the TAU-Lab at Politecnico di Milano. He has been a visiting scholar at Yale, Johns Hopkins, Columbia University, and Sciences Po, and Visiting Professor at TU Munich. He is the coauthor (with photographer Michele Nastasi) of the book *Starchitecture: Scenes, Actors, and Spectacles in Contemporary Cities* (Monacelli Press); coeditor (with Harvey Molotch) of the book *The New Arab Urban: Gulf Cities of Wealth, Ambition, and Distress* (New York University Press); and author of *Transnational Architecture and Urbanism: Rethinking How Cities Plan, Transform, and Learn* (Routledge).

Paolo Scrivano

Paolo Scrivano is Associate Professor of History of Architecture at Politecnico di Milano. He received a PhD from Politecnico di Torino, and has taught at the University of Toronto, Boston University, and Xi'an Jiaotong-Liverpool University. He has been Visiting Fellow at the National Gallery of Art, Visiting Scholar at the Canadian Centre for Architecture, and the Massachusetts Institute of Technology, and has authored the volumes *Storia di un'idea di architettura moderna. Henry-Russell Hitchcock e l'International Style* (Franco Angeli), *Olivetti Builds: Modern Architecture in Ivrea* (Skira; with Patrizia Bonifazio), and *Building Transatlantic Italy: Architectural Dialogues with Postwar America* (Ashgate).

Joachim Thiel

Joachim Thiel is a Senior Lecturer in Social Economic Urban and Regional Research at HafenCity University in Hamburg. In the last decade he has been doing research on large-scale urban development ventures, for instance, on the London Olympics construction program and on six large-scale construction projects in Germany. In addition to that Thiel's research focus has been on creative industries in the urban economy as well as on urban digitalization policies. Thiel is the coeditor of two recent books on large projects published with Jovis.

References

INTRODUCTION

Alaily-Mattar, N., Ponzini, D., & Thierstein, A. (2020, Eds.) *About Star Architecture: Reflecting on Cities in Europe.* Cham: Springer.

Clunn, H. P. (1933a) *The Face of London: The Record of a Century's Changes and Developments.* London: Simpkin Marshall.

Clunn, H. P. (1933b) *The Face of Paris: The Record of a Century's Changes and Developments.* London: Simpkin Marshall.

Farías, I. & Bender, T. (2010, Eds.) *Urban Assemblages: How Actor-Network Theory Changes Urban Studies.* New York: Routledge.

Feininger, A. & Lyman. S. E. (1954) *The Face of New York: The City as It Was and as It Is.* New York: Crown Publishers.

Jacobs, J. M. (2006) "A Geography of Big Things." *Cultural Geographies*, 13(1), 1–27.

Jacobs, J. M. & Merriman, P. (2011) "Practising Architectures." *Social & Cultural Geography,* 12(3), 211–222.

Latour, B. (2005) *Reassembling the Social: An Introduction to Actor-Network-Theory.* Oxford: Oxford University Press.

Lieto, L. & Beauregard, R. A. (2015, Eds.) *Planning for a Material World.* New York: Routledge.

Molotch, H. & Ponzini, D. (2019, Eds.) *The New Arab Urban: Gulf Cities of Wealth, Ambition, and Distress.* New York: New York University Press.

Molotch, H. & Ponzini D. with Nastasi, M. N. (2022) *Seeing through Gulf Cities. Urbanization in and from the Arabian Peninsula.* Trento: ListLab.

Nastasi, M. (2016) "Skyline Rêverie." *Lotus*, 159, 72–87.

Nicolin, P. (2012) *La Verità in Architettura. Il Pensiero di un'Altra Modernità.* Macerata: Quodlibet.

Permasteelisa Group of Companies (1999) *Habitat, Technology and Architectural Envelopes.* 3rd ed.

Vittorio Veneto: Permasteelisa Group.

Ponzini, D. (2020) *Transnational Architecture and Urbanism: Rethinking How Cities Plan, Transform, and Learn.* London: Routledge.

Sklair, L. (2017) *The Icon Project: Architecture, Cities, and Capitalist Globalization.* Oxford: Oxford University Press.

Statista (2022) *Global Business Cities Report.* Retrieved from: https://www.statista.com/study/62120/statista-global-business-cities.

Tafuri, M. (1973) "La Montagna Disincantata. Il Grattacielo e la City." In Ciucci, G., Dal Co, F., Manieri-Elia M., &

Tafuri, M. (Eds.) *La Città Americana dalla Guerra Civile al New Deal.* Rome: Laterza, 417–550.

Quaroni, L. (1954) "Il volto della città." *Comunità* 25, 46-49 [republished in Id. (2019) "I Volti della città." Ivrea: Edizioni di Comunità].

United Nations [Department of Economic and Social Affairs, Population Division] (2018). *World Urbanization Prospects.* New York: United Nations.

Yaneva, A. (2017) *Five Ways to Make Architecture Political: An Introduction to the Politics of Design Practice.* London: Bloomsbury Publishing.

CHAPTER 1

Balke, J., Reuber, P., & Wood, G. (2018) "Iconic Architecture and Place-specific Neoliberal Governmentality: Insights from Hamburg's Elbe Philharmonic Hall." *Urban Studies*, 5, 997–1012.

Ballon, H. & Jackson, K. T. (2007, Eds.) *Robert Moses and the Modern City: The Transformation of New York.* New York: W. W. Norton.

Barjot, D. (1996) "Les industries d'équipement et de la construction." In Lévy-Leboyer, M. (Ed.). *Histoire de la France industrielle.* Paris: Larousse Bordas, 412–433.

Clausen, M. L. (2005) *The Pan Am Building and the Shattering of the Modernist Dream.* Cambridge, MA – London: The MIT Press.

Comba, M. (2011, Ed.) Maire Tecnimont. *I progetti FIAT Engineering.* Cinisello Balsamo: Silvana Editoriale.

Croset, P.-A. (1980, Ed.) "I clienti di Le Corbusier." *Rassegna*, 3.

Dobbels, J. (2021) *Building a Profession: A History of General Contractors in Belgium (1870–1970).* Brussels: VUB Press.

Drexler, A. (1964) *Twentieth-Century Engineering.* New York: The Museum of Modern Art.

Fainstein, S. S. (1994) *The City Builders: Property, Politics, and Planning in London and New York.* Oxford – Cambridge, MA: Blackwell Publishers.

Farías, I. & Bender, T. (2010, Eds.) *Urban Assemblages: How Actor-Network Theory Changes Urban Studies.* Abingdon – New York: Routledge.

Fohlen, C. (1978) "Entrepreneurship and Management in France in the Nineteenth Century." In Mathias, P. & Postan, M. (Eds.) *The Cambridge Economic History of Europe.* Cambridge: Cambridge University Press, 347–381.

Foster, H. (2002) *Design and Crime and Other Diatribes.* London – New York: Verso.

Frank, H. (1993) "La tarda vittoria del Neues Bauen. L'architettura tedesca dopo la seconda guerra mondiale." *Rassegna*, 54, 58–67.

Gagès, P. (1989, Ed.) *L'Avenir Entreprise Coopéra-tive. 70 ans de l'histoire d'une métropole. 70 ans d'ar-chitecture.* Liège: Mardaga.

Hitchcock, H.-R. (1955) *Latin American Architecture: Since 1945.* New York: The Museum of Modern Art.

Hitchcock, H.-R. (1962) "Notes of a Traveller (III): European Skyscrapers." *Zodiac* 9, 4–17.

Jambard, P. (2008) *Un constructeur de la France du XXe siècle. La Société Auxiliaire d'Entreprises (SAE) et la naissance de la grande entreprise française de bâ-timent (1924–1974).* Rennes: Presses Universitaires de Rennes.

James, K. (1997) *Erich Mendelsohn and the Archi-tecture of German Modernism.* New York: Cambridge University Press.

Jannière, H. & Scrivano, P. (2020) "Public Debate and Public Opinion: Notes for a Research on Architectural Criticism." *CLARA Architecture/Recherche* 7, 18–29.

Maniaque, C. (2005) *Le Corbusier et les maisons Jaoul: projets et fabrique.* Paris: Picard, 2005.

Murray, P. (2004, Ed.) *The Saga of Sydney Opera House: The Dramatic Story of the Design and Con-struction of the Icon of Modern Australia.* London – New York: Spoon Press.

Ockman, J. (2004) "New Politics of the Spectacle: 'Bilbao' and the Global Imagination." In Lasansky, D. M. & McLaren, B. (Eds.). *Architecture and Tourism: Perception, Performance, and Place.* Oxford – New York: Berg, 227–239.

Ponzini, D. (2020) *Transnational Architecture and Urbanism: Rethinking How Cities Plan, Transform, and Learn.* Abingdon – New York: Routledge.

Scrivano, P. (2009) "Architecture." In Iriye, A. & Sau-nier, P.-Y. (Eds.). *The Palgrave Dictionary of Transna-tional History.* Houndmills – New York: Palgrave Mac-millan, 53–56.

Scrivano, P. (2012) "The Persistent Success of Bi-ography: Architecture as a Narrative of the Individual." ABE Journal: *European Architecture Beyond Europe.*

Sculpting the Sky: Petronas Twin Towers, KLCC (1998). Kuala Lumpur: Al Hilal.

Spina, D. (2022) "The Bureaucratisation of Archi-tecture in Post-War Italy: SGI under Aldo Samaritani, 1945–73." *Architectural History*, 65, 81–104.

CHAPTER 2

Carpo, M. (2017) *The Second Digital Turn.* Cam-bridge, MA: The MIT Press.

Carpo, M. (2023) *Beyond Digital. Design and Automation at the End of Modernity.* Cambridge, MA: The MIT Press.

Cohen, J. L. (2021). *Frank Gehry. The Masterpieces.* Paris: Cahiers d'Art Flammation.

Permasteelisa Group (2015) *Architectural Enve-lopes.* Vittorio Veneto: Permasteelisa Group.

Venturi, R., (1966) *Complexity and Contradiction in Ar-chitecture.* New York: The Museum of Modern Art.

Zaera-Polo, A. (2006) "Conversations with Frank O. Gehry." *El Croquis*, 45 [Frank O. Gehry 1987–2003], 12–44.

Zaera-Polo A. & Anderson, J. S. (2020) *The Ecolo-gies of the Building Envelope.* Barcelona: Actar.

CHAPTER 3

Alaily-Mattar, N., Ponzini, D., & Thierstein, A. (2020, Eds.) *About Star Architecture: Reflecting on Cities in Europe.* Cham: Springer.

Easterling, K. (2005) *Enduring Innocence: Glob-al Architecture and Its Political Masquerades.* Cam-bridge, MA: The MIT Press.

McNeill, D. (2009) *The Global Architect. Firms, Fame, and Urban Form.* New York: Routledge.

Paoletti, I. (2003) *Una Finestra sul Trasferimento: Tecnologie Innovative per l'Architettura.* Milan: Clup.

Permasteelisa Group of Companies (1999a) *Hab-itat, Technology and Architectural Envelopes*. 3rd ed. Vittorio Veneto: Permasteelisa Group.

Ponzini, D. (2020) *Transnational Architecture and Urbanism: Rethinking How Cities Plan, Transform, and Learn.* London: Routledge.

Sklair, L. (2017) *The Icon Project: Architecture, Cit-ies, and Capitalist Globalization.* New York: Oxford University Press.

CHAPTER 4

Boland Jr, R. J., Lyytinen, K., & Yoo, Y. (2007) "Wakes of Innovation in Project Networks: The Case of Digital 3-D Representations in Architecture, Engineering, and Con-struction". *Organization Science*, 18(4), 631–647.

Bosch, G. & Hüttenhoff, F. (2022) *Der Bauarbeit-smarkt. Soziologie und Ökonomie einer Branche.* [sec-ond edition], Frankfurt/New York: Campus

Bruns-Berentelg, J., Walter J., & Meyhöfer, D. (2012, Eds.). *HafenCity Hamburg. Das erste Jahrzehnt.* Ham-burg: Junius-Verlag.

Butzin, A. & Rehfeld, D. (2013) "The Balance of Change in Continuity in the German Construction Sector's Development Path." *Zeitschrift für Wirtschafts-geographie*, 57(1–2), 15–26.

Davies, A. (2017) *Projects. A Very Short Introduc-tion.* Oxford: Oxford University Press.

Davies, A., MacAulay, S., DeBarro, T., & Thurston, M. (2014) "Making Innovation Happen in a Megaproject:

London's Crossrail Suburban Railway System." *Project Management Journal*, 45(6), 25–37.

Dreher, J. & Thiel, J. (2022) "Star Architecture Projects and the Geographies of Innovation in the Construction Supply Chain: The Case of the Elbphilharmonie." *European Planning Studies*, 30(1), 105–120.

Dreher, J., Thiel, J., Grabher, G., & Grubbauer, M. (2021) "Mobile Interaction, Sticky Products: Geographies of Innovation in Large-Scale Construction Projects." In J. Thiel, V. Dimitrova & J. Ruge (Eds.). *Constructing Innovation: How Large-Scale Projects Drive Novelty in the Construction Industry*. Berlin: Jovis, 86–104.

Mergenthaler, A., Goeddertz, S., Grenz, U., & Strehlke, K. (2010) "A Crystal in the Harbour – The Glass Façade of the Elbphilharmonie." *Detail*, 05/2010, 44–53.

Meyhöfer, D. (2023) *Vom Ort zur Marke. Transformation eines Hamburger Großprojekts*. Berlin: DOM Publishers.

Mischke, Joachim (2017) "Die Architekten." Hamburger Abendblatt, January 1.

Schmaltz, A., Wohlraub, K., Schaller, J., & Mack, T. (2016) *Elbphilharmonie: Von der Vision zur Wirklichkeit. Television Documentation*. NDR Fernsehen Norddeutscher Rundfunk.

Thiel, J., Dimitrova, V., & Ruge, J. (2021, Eds.) *Constructing Innovation: How Large-Scale Projects Drive Novelty in the Construction Industry*. Berlin: Jovis.

CHAPTER 5

Bollani, D. & Masera, G. (2016) "Behind the Curtain Wall," published with *Domus*, 1003, June 2016.

Cornette, D., Georgi, M., & Birken, T. (2018) *Gartner 150 Years*. Vittorio Veneto: Permasteelisa Group.

Dal Co, F. (1991, Ed.) *Padiglione del libro Electa della Biennale di Venezia*. Milan: Electa.

Fromonot, F. (1998) *Jørn Utzon: Architect of the Sydney Opera House*. Milan: electa for Permasteelisa.

Garzia, C. & Moretti, A. (2004) *Massimo Colomban e la Permasteelisa 1974–2002*. Milan: ISEDI.

Permasteelisa (1988) *Quartenario System*. Conegliano: Permasteelisa.

Permasteelisa (1990) *Quaternario 90: International Award for Innovative Technology in Architecture: Permasteelisa Architectural Components*. Venice.

Permasteelisa Group of Companies (1997) *138 Architectural Envelopes and Building Components*. 3rd ed. Vittorio Veneto: Permasteelisa Group of Companies.

Permasteelisa Group of Companies (1999a) *Habitat, Technology and Architectural Envelopes*. 3rd ed. Vittorio Veneto: Permasteelisa Group.

Permasteelisa Group of Companies (1999b) *150 Architectural Envelopes Built by Permasteelisa Group Throughout the World*. Vittorio Veneto: Permasteelisa Group.

Permasteelisa Group (2003) *Architectural Envelopes*. Vittorio Veneto: Permasteelisa Group.

Permasteelisa Group (2011) *Architectural Envelopes*. Vittorio Veneto: Permasteelisa Group.

Permasteelisa Group (2012) *Interiors & Contracts*. Vittorio Veneto: Permasteelisa Group.

Permasteelisa Group (2013) *Airport Terminals*. Vittorio Veneto: Permasteelisa Group.

Permasteelisa Group (2014) *Shape! Bringing Architecture to Life*. Venice: Permasteelisa Group.

Permasteelisa Group (2015) *Architectural Envelopes*. Vittorio Veneto: Permasteelisa Group.

Permasteelisa Group (2017) *Shape! Bringing Architecture to Life*. Exhibition Catalogue.

Permasteelisa Group (2018) *Complexity and Eternal Beauty*. Vittorio Veneto: Permasteelisa Group.

Permasteelisa S.p.a. Italy (2005) *Space and Light: Innovative Architecture in Steel and Glass*. Treviso: Eurocom4.

Vedovato, M., Ministeri, A., & Costantini, A. (2021) "La valutazione del margine delle commesse pluriennali: il caso Permasteelisa Group," *Management Control*, special issue 2, 2021. Milan: Franco Angeli, 215–240.

Photo credits

This book has been realized with the support of the Permasteelisa Group on the occasion of its fiftieth anniversary

www.permasteelisagroup.com
facebook.com/permasteelisagroup
linkedin.com/company/permasteelisa-spa
instagram.com/permasteelisagroup

Edited by
Davide Ponzini
(Politecnico di Milano)
To my daughter Sara, whose gestation ran parallel to the creation of this book

Research Assistance
Marco Antonio Minozzo Gabriel
(Politecnico di Milano)
Zachary Mark Jones
(Politecnico di Milano)

Art Direction and Graphic Design
Martina Toccafondi

Iconographical Research
Marina Itolli

Cartography and Visualization
Propp

FSC
www.fsc.org
MIX
Paper | Supporting
responsible forestry
FSC® C084761

© 2023 Mondadori Libri S.p.A.
Distributed in English throughout the World
by Rizzoli International Publications Inc.
300 Park Avenue South
New York, NY 10010, USA

ISBN: 978-88-918387-5-9

2024 2025 2026 2027 / 10 9 8 7 6 5 4 3 2 1

First edition: March 2024

This volume was printed at O.G.M. S.p.A., Padua

Printed in Italy

Visit us online:
Facebook.com/RizzoliNewYork
Twitter: @Rizzoli_Books
Instagram.com/RizzoliBooks
Pinterest.com/RizzoliBooks
Youtube.com/user/RizzoliNY
Issuu.com/Rizzoli